The Wisdom of
Confucius

The Wisdom of Confucius

A Citadel Press Book

Published by Carol Publishing Group

Carol Publishing Group Edition, 1996
A Citadel Press Book
Published by Carol Publishing Group
Citadel Press is a registered trademark of
Carol Communications, Inc.
For editorial, sales and distribution, and questions regarding
rights and permissions, write to Carol Publishing Group, 120
Enterprise Avenue, Secaucus, NJ 07094
In Canada: Canadian Manda Group, One Atlantic Avenue, Suite
105, Toronto, Ontario, M6K 3E7
Carol Publishing Group Books are available at special discounts
for bulk purchases, for sales promotions, fund-raising, or
educational purposes.
Special editions can be created to specifications.
Designed by Jessica Shatan
Manufactured in the United States of America
12 11 10 9 8 7 6 5 4 3 2 1
Library of Congress Cataloging-in-Publication Data
Confucius.
    [Lun yü. English. Selections]
    The wisdom of Confucius.
       p.   cm.
    "The present selection is taken from The Confucian Analects,
translated by William Jennings."
    Originally published : New York : Philosophical Library, 1968.
    ISBN 0-8065-1702-6 (pbk.)
    I. Jennings, William, 1847–1927. II. Title.
PL2478.L4   1995
181'.112--dc20   95–19792
                                                      CIP

Foreword

Confucius was born in the year 551 B.C. His father was governor of a small district within the present province of Shantung. When Confucius was born his father was rather on in years; as a result, he did not live long enough to know his son's fame.

The name "Confucius" is, of course, not Chinese; it is only the Latinized form of his true name, which was K'ung, and the name Fu-tsz, which means "Master" and was given to him in his manhood.

Like most Chinese, Confucius married at an early age; at nineteen he was a husband and at twenty a father. He had at least one son and one daughter.

There is not much known about Confucius' early years and his education. It is known that at about the time of his marriage he also began to work, assuming a minor administrative position. This sort of work did not satisfy him, however, and after two years he left his position to teach and study. He made such progress in this that his fame spread and men of even higher position came to consult him.

When he was twenty-four, his mother died and he followed the Chinese custom of retiring from active life for three years' mourning. But, although cut off from public life, those three years were fruitful, for he devoted much of his time thinking about how to remedy the state of Chinese government and society. He studied history in order to become a statesman as well as a philosopher, his aim being to reconstruct the moral and material welfare of the people.

By the time he reached the age of 30 Confucius felt he was firmly established in what he had learned, so he began, in an informal manner, to teach. Soon disciples flocked to him, and he became well-known. He also rose in the ranks of the administrative hierarchy until he was appointed Minister of Crime and Chief Judge in his own country of Lu. In this latter position he became somewhat of a national hero; it was said that his very appointment was equivalent to putting an end to crime; there were no cases to try.

However, he was eventually ousted from his judicial position by jealous rivals and spent the rest of his life, somewhat disillusioned, traveling from state to state with a few disciples, lecturing and teaching. He spent the last five years of his life in literary pursuits and died in 478 B.C. at the age of 73.

Contents

ix

The Wisdom of
Confucius

One

Opinions respecting certain of his disciples and others—

Approach of a disciple to the "golden rule"

—Miscellaneous.

1. The Master pronounced Kung-ye Ch'ang (a disciple) to be a marriageable person; for although lying bound in criminal fetters he had committed no crime. And he gave him his own daughter to wife.

Of Nan Yung (a disciple) he observed, that in a State where the government was well conducted he would not be passed over in its appointments, and in one where the government was ill conducted he would evade punishment and disgrace. And he caused his elder brother's daughter to be given in marriage to him.

2. Of Tsz-tsien (a disciple) he remarked, "A superior man indeed is the like of him! (But) had there been none of superior quality in Lu, how should this man have attained to this (excellence)?"

3. Tsz-kung asked, "What of *me*, then?" "You," replied the Master,—"You are a receptacle." "Of

what sort?" said he. "One for high and sacred use,"[1] was the answer.

4. Some one having observed of Yen Yung that he was good-natured towards others, but that he lacked the gift of ready speech, the Master said, "What need of that gift? To stand up before men and pour forth a stream of glib words is generally to make yourself obnoxious to them. I know not about his good-naturedness; but at any rate what need of that gift?"

5. When the Master proposed that Tsi-tiau K'ai should enter the government service, the latter replied, "I can scarcely credit it."—The Master was gratified.

1. A free rendering of 瑚璉, *u lin*, the name of a grain-holder, made of coral or ornamented with gems, and used at the royal sacrifices. Compare this answer of the Master with II. 12; it is complimentary, but does not allow this disciple to consider himself yet perfect.

6. "Good principles are making no progress," once exclaimed the Master. "If I were to take a raft, and drift about on the sea, would Tsz-lu, I wonder, be my follower there?" That disciple was delighted at hearing the suggestion; whereupon the Master continued, "He surpasses me in his love of deeds of daring. But he does not in the least grasp the pith (of my remark)."

7. In reply to a question put to him by Mang Wu respecting Tsz-lu,—as to whether he might be called good-natured towards others,—the Master said, "I cannot tell"; but, on the question being put again, he answered, "Well, in an important State[1] he might be entrusted with the management of the (military) levies; but I cannot answer for his good nature."

"What say you then of Yen Yu?"

"As for Yen," he replied, "in a city of a thousand families, or in a secondary fief,[2] he might be

1. Lit. "a State of 1000 (war) chariots."
2. Lit. "a House of 100 (war) chariots."

charged with the governorship; but I cannot answer for his good-naturedness."

"Take Tsz-hwa, then; what of him?"

"Tsz-hwa," said he, "with a cincture girt upon him, standing (as attendant) at Court, might be charged with the addressing of visitors and guests; but as to his good-naturedness I cannot answer."

8. Addressing Tsz-kung, the Master said, "Which of the two is ahead of the other—yourself or Hwúi?" "How shall I dare," he replied, "even to *look* at Hwúi? Only let him hear one particular, and from that he knows ten; whereas *I*, if I hear one, may from it know two."

"You are not a match for him, I grant you," said the Master. "You are not his match."

9. Tsai Yu (a disciple) used to sleep in the day-time. Said the Master, "One may hardly carve rotten wood, or use a trowel to the wall of a manureyard! In his case, what is the use of reprimand?"

"My attitude towards a man in my first dealings with him," he added, "was to listen to his professions and to trust to his conduct. My attitude now is to listen to his professions, and to *watch* his conduct. My experience with Tsai Yu has led to this change."

10. "I have never seen," said the Master, "a man of inflexible firmness." Some one thereupon mentioned Shin Ch'ang (a disciple). "Ch'ang," said he, "is wanton; where do you get at his inflexibleness?"

11. Tsz-kung made the remark: "That which I do not wish others to put upon me, I also wish not to put upon others."[1] "Nay," said the Master, "*you* have not got so far as that."

1. Here is an approach, on the negative side, to the golden rule. See also Book XII. 2, for a similar approach to it made by Confucius himself; also XV. 23. In view of the frequent quotation of these passages I have deemed it important to be exact about the verbs. Here the word 加, *ka*, is used, meaning to add to, as a burden; in the other passages it is 施, *shi*, to spread out, to display, to set before.

12. The same disciple once remarked, "There may be access so as to hear the Master's literary discourses, but when he is treating of human nature and the way of Heaven, there may not be such access."[1]

13. Tsz-lu, after once hearing him upon some subject, and feeling himself as yet incompetent to carry into practice what he had heard, used to be apprehensive only lest he should hear the subject revived.

14. Tsz-kung asked how it was that Kung Wăn[2] had come to be so styled "Wăn" (the Talented). The Master's answer was, "Because, though a man of an

---

1. Certain deeper subjects were only for those who had "ears to hear."
2. A former high official of the State of Wei. His name had been Kung Yu; the posthumous title of Wăn (the talented or accomplished) had been conferred on him; but there was evidently room for doubt as to whether his whole character deserved it.

active nature, he was yet fond of study, and he was not ashamed to stoop to put questions to his inferiors."

15. Respecting Tsz-ch'an,[1] the Master said that he had four of the essential qualities of the "superior man":—in his own private walk he was humble-minded; in serving his superiors he was deferential; in his looking after the material welfare of the people he was generously kind; and in his exaction of public service from the latter he was just.

16. Speaking of Yen Ping,[2] he said, "He was one who was happy in his mode of attaching men to him. However long the intercourse, he was always deferential to them."

17. Referring to Tsang Wǎn,[3] he asked, "What is to be said of this man's discernment?—this man

1. A great statesman of Confucius' time.
2. Another great officer of the same period.
3. A great officer of Lu, given to superstition.

with his tortoise-house, with the pillar-heads and posts bedizened with scenes of hill and mere!"[1]

18. Tsz-chang put a question relative to the chief Minister (of Tsu), Tsz-wăn. He said, "Three times he became chief Minister, and on none of these occasions did he betray any sign of exultation. Three times his ministry came to an end, and he showed no sign of chagrin. He used without fail to inform the new Minister as to the old mode of administration. What say you of *him*?"

"That he was a loyal man," said the Master.

"But was he a man of fellow-feeling?" said the disciple.

"Of that I am not sure," he answered; "how am I to get at *that*?"

(The disciple went on to say):—"After the assassination of the prince of Ts'i by the officer Ts'ui, the

1. Properly water-grass: and altogether more strictly, "His pillar-heads representing hills, and the king-posts of the roof water-grass."

10

latter's fellow-official Ch'in Wăn, who had half a score teams of horses, gave up all, and turned his back upon him. On coming to another State, he observed, "There are here characters somewhat like that of our minister Ts'ui," and he turned his back upon *them*. Proceeding to a certain other State, he had occasion to make the same remark, and left. What say you of *him*?"

"That he was a pure-minded man," answered the Master.

"But was he a man of fellow-feeling?" urged the disciple.

"Of that I am not sure," he replied; "how am I to get at that?"

19. Ki Wăn[1] was one who thought three times over a thing before he acted. The Master hearing this of him, observed, "Twice would have been enough."

1. An officer of Lu.

20. Of Ning Wu,[1] the Master said that when matters went well in the State he used to have his wits about him: but when they went wrong, he lost them. His *intelligence* might be equalled, but not his witlessness!

21. Once, when the Master lived in the State of Ch'in, he exclaimed, "Let me get home again! Let me get home! My school-children[2] are wild and impetuous! Though they are *somewhat* accomplished, and perfect in one sense in their attainments, yet they know not how to make nice discriminations."

22. Of Pĕh-I and Shuh Ts'i[3] he said, "By the fact of their not remembering old grievances, they gradually did away with resentment."

1. An officer of Wei, a century before the Sage's time.
2. A familiar way of speaking of his disciples in their hearing.
3. A celebrated pair of brothers—princes—who lived in the latter part of the twelfth century B.C. As we shall meet with their names two or three times more, some account of them may be given here. Their father was feudal prince of a small State dur-

23. Of Wei-shang Kau[1] he said, "Who calls him straightforward? A person once begged some vinegar of him, and he begged it from a *neighbor*, and then presented him with it!"

24. "Fine speech," said he, "and studied mien, and superfluous show of deference,—of such things Tso-k'iu Ming[2] was ashamed. I too am ashamed of such things. Also of hiding resentment felt towards

ing the reign of the last king of the Yin dynasty, and he desired to make the younger of them his successor. But nothing would induce the younger brother to supplant the elder, and he fled the country on his father's death. The elder in turn declined the heirship, and also retired, leaving the throne to a third brother. They emerged from their retreat in their old age, to find a change in the dynasty, and refusing allegiance to the House of Chow they retired again to a mountain district, lived as they could on wild fruits, and finally died of starvation. Their faithfulness to each other and their steadfast adherence to what they considered a duty is praised both by Confucius and Mencius.

1. A man of Lu, well known for his straightforwardness and honesty.
2. Some celebrity of older times.

an opponent and treating him as a friend—of *this* kind of thing he was ashamed, and so too am I."

25. Attended once by the two disciples Yen Yuen[1] and Tsz-lu, he said, "Come now, why not tell me, each of you, what in your hearts you are really after?"

"I should like," said Tsz-lu, "for myself and my friends and associates, carriages and horses, and to be clad in light furs! nor would I mind much if they should become the worse for wear. "[2]

"And I should like," said Yen Yuen, "to live without boasting of my abilities, and without display of meritorious deeds."

Tsz-lu then said, "I should like, sir, to hear what *your* heart is set upon."

1. *Alias* Hwúi.
2. This may seem childish, but it is evidently a circumlocution for "I would like, for my friends and self, some high official grade, and would use my dignity, if necessary with economy. Cf. *Shi-King*, I. ii. 7; I. xiii. I (notes).

14

The Master replied, "It is this:—in regard to old people, to give them quiet and comfort; in regard to friends and associates, to be faithful to them; in regard to the young, to treat them with fostering affection and kindness."

26. On one occasion the Master exclaimed, "Ah, 'tis hopeless![1] I have not yet seen the man who can see his errors, so as inwardly to accuse himself."

27. "In a small cluster of houses[2] there may well be," said he, "some whose integrity and sincerity may compare with mine; but I yield to none in point of love of learning."

1. Or, "all is over!"
2. Lit. in a group of ten families.

Two

More characteristics of disciples—*"Obiter dicta"*—Wisdom—Philanthropy.

1. Of (Yen) Yung (a disciple) the Master said, "Yung might indeed do for a prince!" [1]

On being asked by this Yen Yung[2] his opinion of a certain individual,[3] the Master replied, "He is passable. Impetuous, (though)."

"But," argued the disciple, "if a man habituate himself to a reverent regard for duty—even while in his way of doing things he is impetuous—in the oversight of the people committed to his charge, is he not passable? If, on the other hand, he habituate himself to impetuosity of mind, and show it also in his way of doing things, is he not then *over*impetuous?"

"You are right," said the Master.

---

1. Lit. "for a *south-facer*." It was then and is still the custom for persons of royal rank to sit facing the south. Yen Yung was one of the most approved of the Sage's disciples.
2. Chung Kung, in the original; but this was only the posthumous title of the Yen Yung just mentioned; and I think it better to avoid confusion in these names. The same remark applies to parag. 4.
3. Tsz-sang Peh-tsz, in the original; evidently some official; but as nothing is known of him, the name, uncouth enough to English ears, is surely better omitted.

19

2. When the duke Ngai inquired which of the disciples were devoted to learning, Confucius answered him, "There was one Yen Hwúi who loved it,—a man whose angry feelings towards any particular person he did not suffer to visit upon another; a man who would never fall into the same error twice. Unfortunately his allotted time was short, and he died, and now his like is not to be found; I have never heard of one (so) devoted to learning."

3. While Tsz-hwa (a disciple) was away on a mission to Ts'i, the disciple Yen Yu on behalf of his mother applied for some grain. "Give her three pecks," said the Master. He applied for more. "Give her eight, then." Yen gave her fifty times that amount.—The Master said, "When Tsz-hwa[1] went on that journey to Ts'i, he had well-fed steeds yoked to his carriage, and was arrayed in light furs. I have learnt that the 'superior man' should help those

1. Ch'ih, in original; but only another name for the same man.

whose needs are urgent, not help the rich to be more rich."

When Yuen Sz became prefect under him, he gave him nine hundred measures of grain, but the prefect declined to accept them.[1] "You must not," said the Master. "May they not be of use to the villages and hamlets around you?"

4. Speaking of Yen Yung (again), the Master said, "If the offspring of a speckled ox be red in colour, and horned, even though men may not wish to take it (for sacrifice), would (the spirits of) the hills and streams reject it?"[2]

1. At this time Confucius was Criminal Judge in his native State of Lu. Yuen Sz had been a disciple. The commentators add that this was the officer's proper salary, and that he did wrong to refuse it.

2. Yen Yung had a bad father, and men were inclined to avoid him on that account. Hence this remark made on his behalf. Oxen acceptable for sacrifice were required to be red and horned.

5. Adverting to Hwúi again, he said, "For three months there would not be in his breast one thought recalcitrant against his feeling of goodwill towards his fellow-men. The others may attain to this for a day or for a month, but there they end."

6. When asked by Ki K'ang[1] whether Tsz-lu was fit to serve the government, the Master replied, "Tsz-lu is a man of *decision:* what should prevent him from serving the government?"

Asked the same question respecting Tsz-(kung) and Yen Yu he answered similarly, pronouncing Tsz-kung to be a man of *perspicacity,* and Yen Yu to be one *versed in the polite arts.*

1. Ki K'ang was head of one of the "Three Families" of Lu. He inquires respecting the qualifications of these disciples for office. The questions are put separately about each, and are formally answered separately by the Master, as if by way of *certificate.*

7. When the head of the Ki family sent for Min Tsz-k'ien to make him governor of (the town of) Pi, that disciple said, "Politely decline for me. If the offer is renewed, then indeed I shall feel myself obliged to go and live on the (further) bank of the Wăn."[1]

8. Peh-niu[2] had fallen ill, and the Master was inquiring after him. Taking hold of his hand (held out) from the window, he said, "It is taking him off! Alas, his appointed time has come! Such a man, and to have such an illness!"

1. Min Tsz-k'ien was one of the Sage's favourite disciples, and he, no more than his master, could brook the manners of the Ki family. On the further bank of the Wăn he would be out of the territory, and free from further solicitation.
2. Another favourite disciple. He was suffering, it is thought, from leprosy.

9. Of Hwúi (again): "A right worthy man indeed was he! With his simple wooden dish of rice, and his one gourd-basin of drink, away in his poor back lane, in a condition too grievous for others to have endured, he never allowed his cheery spirits to droop. Ay, a right worthy soul was he!"

10. "It is not," Yen Yu once apologized, "that I do not take pleasure in your doctrines; it is that I am not strong enough." The Master rejoined, "It is when those who are not strong enough have made some moderate amount of progress that they fail and give up; but you are now drawing your own line for yourself."

11. Addressing Tsz-hiá, the Master said, "Let your scholarship be that of gentlemen, and not like that of common men."[1]

1. I. e. seeking self-improvement for its own sake and for duty's sake, not from motives of material benefit.

12. When Tsz-yu became governor of Wu-shing, the Master said to him, "Do you find (good) men about you?" The reply was, "There is Tan-t'ai Mieh-ming,[1] who when walking eschews bye-paths, and who, unless there be some public function, never approaches my private residence."

13. "Mang Chi-fan"[2] said the Master, "is no sounder of his own praises. During a stampede he was in the rear, and as they were about to enter the city gate he whipped up his horses, and said, ' 'Twas not my *daring* made me lag behind. My horses would not go.'"

Obiter dicta of the Master:—

1. This description of him would hardly have been recorded if it did not contain more than appears on the surface. The *quondam* disciple pursues open and plain courses, and knows also how to mind his own business.
2. An officer of Lu.

14. "Whoever has not the glib utterance of the priest T'o, as well as the handsomeness of (prince) Cháu of Sung, will find it hard to keep out of harm's way in the present age.

15. "Who can go out but by (that) door? Why walks no one by these guiding principles?[1]

16. "Where plain naturalness is more in evidence than polish, we have—the man from the country. Where polish is more in evidence than naturalness, we have—the (town) scribe. It is when naturalness and polish are equally evident that we have the ideal man.

17. "The life of a man is—his rectitude. Life *without* it—such may you have the good fortune to avoid![2]

1. Evidently spoken in some room where he customarily gave instruction, and from which there was no *other* exit but by the door.
2. I would ask the attention of critics to this rendering of a

18. "They who know it[1] are not as those who love it, nor they who love it as those who rejoice in it [i. e. have the fruition of their love for it].

19. "To the average man, and those above the average, it is possible to discourse on higher subjects; to those from the average downwards, it is not possible."

20. Fan Ch'i put a query about wisdom. The Master replied, "To labour for the promoting of

rather knotty saying: 人 之 生 也, 直, 罔 之 生 也, 幸 而 免 "Life" is here explained in the Commentaries as "the rational principle underlying life" 生 理 本.
[Since the above was written, a Chinese friend has sent me the following free rendering: "Man is born upright. If he can exist without uprightness his existence is fortunate"; and he adds in a note that "when Confucius says this, he refers to the goodness of God in allowing such people (without uprightness) to exist in the world, and in giving them a larger space for repentance." My friend does not translate the last character 免, to avoid, or escape.]
1. The "it" must, I think, refer to some subject under discussion at the time.

righteous conduct among the people of the land; to be serious in regard to spiritual beings, and to hold aloof[1] from them;—this may be called wisdom."

To a further query, about philanthropy, he replied, "Those who possess that virtue find difficulty with it at first, success later."[2]

21. "Men of practical knowledge," he said, "find their gratification among the rivers (of the lowland), men of sympathetic social feeling find theirs among the hills. The former are active and bustling, the latter calm and quiet. The former take their (day of) pleasure, the latter look to length of days."

22. Alluding to the States of Ts'i and Lu, he observed, that Ts'i, by one change, might attain to the

1. I. e. probably, not to be too familiar, to show reverence from a distance.
2. An unsatisfactory answer, and evasive; unless it be that it was in reply to a particular question about its *exercise*. But he was slow to speak on this subject.

condition of Lu; and that Lu, by one change, might attain to good government.[1]

23. An exclamation of the Master [satirizing the times, when old terms relating to government were still used while bereft of their old meaning]:—"A quart, and not a quart![2] *quart*, indeed! *quart*, indeed!"

24. Tsai Wo (a disciple) put a query. Said he "Suppose a philanthropic person were told, 'There's a fellow-creature down in the well!' Would he go down after him?"

"Why should he really do so?" answered the Master. "The good man [or, a superior man] might be

1. The "one change" would be, in each case, a reform in the direction of the "Proprieties." Tsi was even worse than Lu.
2. The word means really an angular cup, or perhaps a horn-cup, at that time made *without* the angles, or *not* of horn. The meaning will come home to English readers in the above translation. Times are changed even with ourselves as regards such things, and such things are *signs* of the times.

induced to go, but not to go *down*. He may be mis-
led, but not befooled."[1]

25. "The superior man," said he, "with his wide
study of books, and hedging himself round by the
Rules of Propriety, is not surely, after all that, capable of overstepping his bounds."

26. Once when the Master had had an interview
with Nan-tsz,[2] which had scandalized his disciple
Tsz-lu, he uttered the solemn abjuration, "If I have
done aught amiss, may Heaven reject me! may
Heaven reject me!

1. Of course men are liable to practical jokes. The question here
is how far *impulses* will carry different men. The philanthropic
person who is a "superior man" will not be caught napping.
2. The duchess of Wei, who had been guilty of criminal intercourse with her brother, the prince Cháu (of paragraph 14).

27. "How far-reaching," said he, "is the moral excellence that flows from the 'Constant Mean!'[1] It has for a long time been rare among the people."

28. Tsz-kung said, "Suppose the case of one who confers benefits far and wide upon the people, and who can, in so doing, make his bounty universally felt,—how would you speak of him? Might he be called philanthropic?"

The Master exclaimed, "What a work for philanthropy! He would require indeed to be a sage! He would put into shade even Yau and Shun!—Well, a philanthropic person, desiring for *himself* a firm footing, is led on to give one to others; desiring for *himself* an enlightened perception of things, he is led on to help others to be similarly enlightened.— If one could take an illustration coming closer

1. The doctrine afterwards known by that name, and which gave its title to a Confucian treatise.

home to us (than yours), *that* might be made the starting point for speaking about philanthropy."[1]

1. I cannot conceive how Dr. Legge has been able to translate this last sentence thus: "*To be able to judge (of others) by what is nigh (in ourselves),—this may be called the art of virtue.*" Had he forgotten his *Shi-King* (III. iii. 2, last stanza)? 近取譬 here is the same as 取譬不遠 there = "Take an illustration not far-fetched."

Three

Chiefly characteristics of Confucius himself—What he thought of himself—And what others thought—An incident during a time of sickness.

Said the Master:

1. "I, as a transmitter[1] and not an originator, and as one who believes in and loves the ancients, venture to compare myself with our old P'ang.[2]

2. "What find you indeed in *me?*—a quiet brooder and memorizer; a student never satiated with learning; an unwearied monitor of others!

3. "The things which weigh heavily upon my mind are these—failure to improve in the virtues, failure in discussion of what is learnt, inability to walk according to knowledge received as to what is right and just, inability also to reform what has been amiss."

1. In reference to his editing the six Classics of his time.
2. It is uncertain who this was. The "our" is said to indicate endearment or familiarity: he was some worthy known to himself and his disciples, of *very great age.*

4. In his hours of recreation and refreshment the Master's manner was easy and unconstrained, affable and winning.

5. Once he exclaimed, "Alas! I must be getting very feeble: 'tis long since I have had a repetition of the dreams in which I used to see the Duke of Chow."[1]

6. "Concentrate the mind," said he, "upon the Good Way.

"Maintain firm hold upon Virtue.

"Rely upon Philanthropy.

1. This was one of his "beloved ancients," famous for what he did in helping to found the dynasty of Chow, a man of great political wisdom, a scholar also and poet. It was the "dream" of Confucius' life to restore the country to the condition in which the duke of Chow left it.

"Find recreation in the Arts."[1]

7. "I have never withheld instruction from any, even from those who have come for it with the smallest offering" [lit. with their packets of dried meat].

8. "No subject do I broach (however) to those who have no eager desire (to learn); no encouraging hint do I give to those who show no anxiety to speak out their ideas; nor have I anything more to say to those who, after I have made clear one corner of the subject, cannot from that give me the other three."

9. "If the Master was taking a meal, and there were any in mourning beside him, he would not eat to the full.

1. These were six in number, viz. Ceremonial, Music, Archery, Horsemanship, Language, and Calculation.

On one day on which he had wept, on that day he would not sing.

10. Addressing his favourite disciple,[1] he said, "To you only and myself it has been given to do this,—to go when called to serve, and to go back into quiet retirement when released from office."

Tsz-lu (hearing the remark) said, "But if, sir, you had the handling of the army of one of the greater States,[2] whom would you have associated with you in *that*[3] case?"

The Master answered:—

"Not the one 'who'll rouse the tiger,'
Not the one 'who'll wade the Ho';[4]

1. Yen Yuen is the name given, *alias* Hwúi, always spoken of in terms of highest praise.
2. Lit. three forces. Each force consisted of 12,500 men, and three of such forces were the equipment of a greater State.
3. Tsz-lu, the ardent, here shows his jealousy, and is again rebuked.
4. Quotation from *Shi-King*, II. v. 1, last stanza.

not the man who can die with no regret. He must be one who should watch over affairs with apprehensive caution, a man fond of strategy, and of perfect skill and effectiveness in it."

11. As to wealth, he remarked, "If wealth were an object that I *could* go in quest of, I should do so even if I had to take a whip and do grooms' work. But seeing that it is not, I go after those objects for which I have a liking."

12. Among matters over which he exercised great caution were (times of) fasting, war, and sickness.

13. When he was in the State of Ts'i, and had heard the (ancient) Shau music, he lost all perception of the taste of his meat. "I had no idea," said he, "that music could have been brought to this pitch."

14. (In the course of conversation) Yen Yu said, "Does the Master take the part of the prince of Wei?"[1] "Ah yes!" said Tsz-kung, "I will go and ask him that."

On going in to him, that disciple began, "What sort of men were Pĕh-I and Shuh Ts'i?" "Worthies of the olden time," the Master replied. "Had they any feelings of resentment?" was the next question. "Their aim and object," he answered, "was that of doing the duty which every man owes to his fellows, and they succeeded in doing it;—what room further for feelings of resentment?"—The questioner on coming out said, "The Master does not take his part."

15. "With a meal of coarse rice," said the Master, "and with water to drink, and my bent arm for my

1. The prince of Wei was resisting his father's claim to the dukedom. The father had had to flee the country, and the son had thereupon succeeded to the title. Now the father had come back. The question is, Should the son resist the father?

40

pillow,—even *thus* I can find happiness. Riches and honours without righteousness are to me as fleeting clouds."

16. "Give me several years more to live," said he, "and after fifty years' study of the *Book of Changes*[1] I might come to be free from serious error."

17. The Master's regular[2] subjects of discourse were the *Books of the Odes* and *History*, and the up-keeping of the Rules of Propriety. On all of these he regularly discoursed.

18. The duke of Shih questioned Tsz-lu about Confucius, and the latter did not answer.

1. The *Yih-King*.
2. I submit this rendering of 雅 to Chinese scholars who are divided between the commentators' 常 and 正. Kang Hi's Dictionary gives both meanings for the passage, but will not decide.

(Hearing of this), the Master said, "Why did you not say, 'He is a man with a mind so intent on his pursuits that he forgets his food, and finds such pleasure in them that he forgets his troubles, and does not know that old age is coming upon him?' "

19. "As I came not into life with any knowledge of it," he said, "and as my likings are for what is old, I busy myself in seeking knowledge there."

20. Strange occurrences, exploits of strength, deeds of lawlessness, references to spiritual beings,[1]—such-like matters the Master avoided in conversation.

1. Yet once he is represented as saying this of them: "How abundantly do spiritual beings display their influence! We look for them, but do not see them; we hearken to them, but do not hear them; all nature is full of them and nothing can be without them"; and so on.—*Doctrine of the Mean*, chapter xvi.

21. "Let there," he said, "be three men walking together: from that number I should be sure to find my instructors; for what is good in them I should choose out and follow, and what is not good I should modify."

22. On one occasion he exclaimed, "Heaven begat Virtue in me; what can man[1] do unto me?"

23. To his disciples he once said, "Do you look upon me, my sons, as keeping anything secret from you? I hide nothing from you. I do nothing that is not manifest to your eyes, my disciples. That is so with me."

24. Four things there were which he kept in view in his teaching,—scholarliness, conduct of life, honesty, faithfulness.

1. Lit. Hwan T'úi. Hwan T'úi was an officer of Sung, who once set upon him as he was teaching under a tree.

25. "It is not given to me," he said, "to meet with a sage; let me but behold a man of superior mind, and that will suffice. Neither is given to me to meet with a good man; let me but see a man of constancy, and it will suffice.—It is difficult for persons to have constancy, when they pretend to have that which they are destitute of, to be full when they are empty, to do things on a grand scale when their means are contracted!"

26. When the Master fished with hook and line, he did not also use a net. When out with his bow, he would never shoot at game in cover.

27. "Some there may be," said he, "who do things in ignorance of what they do. I am not of these. There is an alternative way of knowing things, viz.—to sift out the *good* from the many things one hears, and follow it; and to keep in memory the many things one sees."

28. (Pupils from) Hu-hiang were difficult to speak with. One youth came to interview the Master, and the disciples were in doubt (whether he ought to have been seen). "Why so much ado," said the Master, "at my merely permitting his approach, and not rather at my allowing him to draw back? If a man have cleansed himself in order to come and see me, I receive him as such; but I do not undertake for what he will do when he goes away."

29. "Is the philanthropic spirit far to seek, indeed?" the Master exclaimed; "I wish for it, and it is with me!"

30. The Minister of Crime in the State of Ch'in asked Confucius whether duke Ch'au (of Lu) was acquainted with the Proprieties; and he answered, "Yes, he knows them."

When Confucius had withdrawn, the minister bowed to Wu-ma K'i (a disciple), and motioned to him to come forward. He said, "I have heard that superior men show no partiality; are *they*, too, then, partial? That prince took for his wife a lady of the Wu family, having the same surname as himself,[1] and had her named "Lady *Tsz* of Wu, the elder." If *he* knows the Proprieties, then who does not?"

The disciple reported this to the Master, who thereupon remarked, "Well for me! If I err in any way, others are sure to know of it."

31. When the Master was in company with any one who sang, and who sang well, he must needs have the song over again, and after that would join in it.

32. "Although in letters," he said, "I may have none to compare with me, yet in my personifica-

---

1. The surname 姬, *Ki*. It was not then, and is not now, allowable in China for persons of the same surname to intermarry, no matter how distantly related. And these surnames were few in comparison with those of Western countries.

tion of the "superior man" I have not as yet been successful."

33. " 'A Sage and a Philanthropist?' How should I have the ambition?" said he. "All that I can well be called is this,—An insatiable student, an unwearied teacher;—this, and no more."—"Exactly what we, your disciples, cannot by any learning manage to be," said Kung-si Hwa.

34. Once when the Master was seriously ill, Tsz-lu requested to be allowed to say prayers for him. "Are such available?" asked the Master.

"Yes," said he; "and the Manual of Prayers[1] says, 'Pray to the spirits above and to those here below.' "

1. It is not precisely known what this collection of Prayers was. They seem to have been more of the nature of eulogies for the departed, and this disciple, forward as ever, seems to have anticipated his master's death. Noteworthy is the Sage's answer, meaning, "My *life* has been a prayer." It was true, and yet it savours a little of self-satisfaction.

"My praying has been going on a long while," said the Master.

35. "Lavish living," he said, "renders men disorderly; miserliness makes them hard. Better, however, the hard than the disorderly."

36. Again, "The man of superior mind is placidly composed; the small-minded man is in a constant state of perturbation."

37. The Master was gentle, yet could be severe; had an over-awing presence, yet was not violent; was deferential, yet easy.

Four

Miscellaneous—Sayings of Tsăng—
Sentences of the Master—Characters of
ancient worthies.

1. Speaking of T'ai-pih[1] the Master said that he might be pronounced a man of the highest moral excellence; for he allowed the empire to pass by him onwards to a third heir; while the people (in their ignorance of his motives) were unable to admire him for so doing.

2. "Without the Proprieties," said the Master, "we have these results: for deferential demeanour, a worried one; for calm attentiveness, awkward bashfulness; for manly conduct, disorderliness; for straightforwardness, perversity.

1. Hereby hangs a historical tale. T'ai-pih lived during the decline of the Yin dynasty. He was eldest son and heir of the ruler of the feudal State of Chow. He had two brothers, upon the younger of whom (the youngest of the three) his father wished the succession to devolve. In order not to stand in the way of that wish, he induced his second brother to go away with him from the country, thus leaving the youngest free. The youngest was named Ki, and he became the father of the renowned Wǎn-wong (King Wǎn), who was the first *virtual* ruler of the new dynasty of Chow. Hence the "empire" really passed out of T'ai-pih's grasp over two brothers to his nephew.

"When men of rank show genuine care for those nearest to them in blood, the people rise to the duty of neighbourliness and sociability. And when old friendships among them are not allowed to fall off, there will be a cessation of underhand practices among the people."

3. The Scholar Tsăng was once unwell, and calling his pupils to him he said to them,

"Disclose to view my feet and my hands. What says the *Ode*?—

> "Act as from a sense of danger,
> With precaution and with care,
> As a yawning gulf o'erlooking,
> As on ice that scarce will bear."

At all times, my children, I know how to keep myself free from (bodily) harm."[1]

1. A lesson on filial duty, best understood by a Chinaman. Our parents gave us our bodies, and they should therefore be carefully guarded from harm. "See mine," says Tsăng, "in my old

4. Again, during an illness of his, Mang King, an official, went to ask after him. The Scholar had some conversation with him, in the course of which he said—

"Doleful the cries of a dying bird,
Good the last words of a dying man."

"There are three points which a man of rank in the management of his duties should set store upon:— A lively manner and deportment, banishing both severity and laxity; a frank and open expression of countenance, allied closely with sincerity; and a tone in his utterances utterly free from any approach to vulgarity and impropriety. As to matters of bowls and dishes,[1] leave such things to those who are charged with the care of them."

age." The lines he quotes are from the *Shi-King*, II. v. 1.
1. In the original the names of *sacrificial* vessels are mentioned, but the lesson is simply, Leave minor matters to those you entrust with them. A Chinese cook some years ago gave this lesson to a Governor of Hong-Kong. The Governor was apt to pay surprise visits to the offices of the various departments, and pry into details of work done. One day he went down into

53

5. Another saying of the Scholar Tsăng:—"I once had a friend[1] who, though he possessed ability, would go questioning men of *none*, and, though surrounded by numbers, would go with his questions to isolated individuals; who also, whatever he might have, appeared as if he were without it, and, with all his substantial acquirements, made as though his mind were a mere blank; and when insulted would not retaliate;—this was ever his way."

6. Again he said:—"The man that is capable of being entrusted with the charge of a minor on the throne, and given authority over a large territory, and who during the important term of his superintendence cannot be forced out of his position,—is not such a 'superior man'? That he is indeed."

his own kitchen to lecture his chief cook. Said the cook, "Sir, you number one governor, I number one cook: you mindee your pidgin (business), I mindee mine." ("Number one" = first-class.)

1. Supposed to be Hwúi.

7. Again:—"The learned official must not be without breadth and power of endurance: the burden is heavy, and the way is long.

"Suppose that he take his duty to his fellow-men as his peculiar burden, is that not indeed a heavy one? And since only with death it is done with, is not the way long?"

Sentences of the Master:—

8. "From the *Book of Odes* (we receive) impulses,
from the *Book of the Rules,* stability,
from the *Book on Music,* refinement.[1]

9. "The people may be put into the way they should go, though they may not be put into the way of understanding it.

1. Comparison of three of the Classics: the *Shi-King,* the *Li Ki,* and the *Yoh.* The last is lost.

10. "The man who likes bravery, and yet groans under poverty, has mischief[1] in him. So, too, has the misanthrope, groaning at any severity shown towards him.

11. "Even if a person were adorned with the gifts of the duke of Chow, yet if he were proud and avaricious, all the rest of his qualities would not indeed be worth looking at.

12. "Not easily found is the man who, after three years' study, has failed to come upon some fruit (of his toil).

13. "The really faithful lover of learning holds fast to the Good Way till death.

"He will not go into a State in which a downfall is imminent, nor take up his abode in one where disorder reigns. When the empire is well ordered he

1. Lit. disorder.

will show himself; when not, he will hide himself away. Under a good government it will be a disgrace to him if he remain in poverty and low estate; under a bad one it would be equally disgraceful to him to hold riches and honours.

14. "If not occupying the office, devise not the policy.

15. "When the professor Chi began his duties, how grand the *finale* of the First of the Odes used to be! How it rang in one's ears!

16. "I cannot understand persons who are enthusiastic and yet not straightforward; nor those who are ignorant and yet not attentive; nor again those folks who are simple-minded and yet untrue.

17. "Learn, as if never overtaking your object, and yet as if apprehensive of losing it.

18. "How sublime was the handling of the empire by Shun and Yu![1]—it was as nothing to them!

19. "How great was Yau as a prince! Was he not sublime! Say that Heaven only is great, then was Yau alone after its pattern! How profound was he! The people could not find a name for him. How sublime in his achievements! How brilliant in his scholarly productions!"

20. "Shun had for his ministers five men, by whom he ordered the empire.

King Wu (in his day) stated that he had ten men as assistants for the promotion of order.

(With reference to these facts) Confucius observed, "Ability is hard to find. Is it not so indeed?

1. These two and Yau (next paragraph) were emperors of the legendary period:—
Yau, B.C. 2356–2258;
Shun, B.C. 2255–2205;
Yu (the Great), founder of the Hia dynasty, B.C. 2205–2197.

During the (three years') interregnum between Yau and Shun there was more of it than in the interval before this present dynasty appeared. There were (at this latter period) one woman, and nine men only.

"When two-thirds of the empire were held (by King Wăn), he served with that portion the House of Yin. (We speak of) the virtue of the House of Chow; we may say indeed that it reached the pinnacle of excellence."

21. "As to Yu," added the Master, "I can find no flaw in him. Living on meagre food and drink; yet providing to the utmost in his filial (offerings) to the spirits (of the dead)! Dressing in coarse garments; yet most elegant when vested in his sacrificial apron and coronet! Dwelling in a poor palace; yet exhausting his energies over those boundary-ditches and watercourses![1] I can find no flaw in Yu."

1. It was these labours for the proper irrigation of the soil and the controlling of inundations that gave him his greatest celebrity.

Five

More sayings respecting himself—His favourite disciple's opinion of him and of his doctrines—Another incident during a serious illness—"*Debetur puero reverentia*"—Miscellaneous.

1. Topics on which the Master rarely spoke were—Advantage, and Destiny, and Duty[1] of man to man.

2. A man of the village of Tah-hiang exclaimed of him, "A great man is Confucius!—a man of extensive learning, and yet in nothing has he quite made himself a name!"

The Master heard of this, and mentioning it to his disciples, he said, "What then shall I take in hand? Shall I become a carriage-driver, or an archer? Let me be a driver!"

3. "The (sacrificial) cap," he once said, "should, according to the Rules, be of linen; but in these days it is of pure silk. However, as it is economical, I do as all do.

"The Rule says, "Make your bow when at the lower end of the hall"; but nowadays the bowing is

1. At any rate a good deal is here *recorded*.

done at the upper part. This is great freedom; and I, though I go in *opposition* to the crowd, bow when at the lower end."

4. The Master barred four (words);—he would have no "shall"s, no "must"s, no "certainly"s, no "I"s.[1]

5. Once, in the town of K'wang, fearing (that his life was going to be taken), the Master exclaimed, "King Wăn is dead and gone; but is not "wăn"[2] with

[1] I believe I am alone in this method of interpretation; but think I am right. The teaching is against arbitrariness, obstinacy, and self-assertion. The last expression is literally "no I's." There is nothing in the Chinese language equivalent to our inverted commas. See also next paragraph.

[2] "Wăn" was the honorary appellation of the great sage and ruler, whose praise is in the *Shi-King* as one of the founders of the Chow dynasty, and the term represented civic talent and virtues, as distinct from Wu, the martial talent—the latter being the honorary title of his son and successor. "Wăn" also often stands for literature, polite accomplishments, *literae humaniores*. Here Confucius simply means, "If you kill me, you kill a sage," &c.

you here? If Heaven be about to allow this "wăn" to perish, then they who survive *its* decease will get no benefit from it. But so long as Heaven does not allow it to perish, what can the men of K'wang do to me?"

6. A high State official, after questioning Tszkung, said, "Your Master is a sage, then? How many and what varied abilities must be his!"

The disciple replied, "Certainly Heaven is allowing him full opportunities of becoming a sage, in addition to the fact that his abilities *are* many and varied."

When the Master heard of this he remarked, "Does that high official know me? In my early years my position in life was low, and *hence* my ability in many ways, though exercised in trifling matters. In the *gentleman* is there indeed such variety (of ability)? No."

(From this, the disciple) Lau used to say, " 'Twas a saying of the Master: 'At a time when I was not called upon to use them, I acquired my proficiency in the polite arts'."

7. "Am *I*, indeed," said the Master, "possessed of knowledge? I know nothing. Let a vulgar fellow come to me with a question,—a man with an emptyish head,—I may thrash out with him the matter from end, and exhaust myself in doing it!"

8. "Ah!" exclaimed he once, "the phoenix does not come! and no symbols issue from the river![1] May I not as well give up?"

---

1. These birds, in Chinese fable and poetry were supposed to appear as the harbingers of good, when virtuous men were numerous, and when the empire was about to become prosperous. See *Shi-King*, III. iii. 8.

The "symbols from the river" have reference also to an ancient fable, in which a dragon-horse emerged from the water with symbolic outlines on his back,—lines which first suggested to the Emperor Fuh-hi the eight mystic diagrams, afterwards the subject of the obscure Classic—the *Yih King*, or *Book of Changes*. No such omens of good, no such revelations from the spirit-world, *now!* Confucius does not necessarily show that he believed in such fables.

9. Whenever the Master met with a person in mourning, or with one in full-dress cap and kirtle, or with a blind person, although they might be *young* persons, he would make a point of rising on their appearance, or, if crossing their path, would do so with quickened step![1]

10. Once Yen Yuen[2] exclaimed with a sigh, (with reference to the Master's doctrines), "If I look up to them, they are ever the higher; if I try to penetrate them, they are ever the harder; if I gaze at them as if before my eyes, lo, they are behind me!—Gradually and gently the Master with skill lures men on. By literary lore he gave me breadth; by the Rules of Propriety he narrowed me down.—When I desire a respite, I find it impossible; and after I have ex-

1. This, in each case, to show his respect or sympathy. The "mourning" should be, more strictly, *half-mourning*, or, mourning attire long worn. The "cap and kirtle" should also be cap, robe, and skirt, denoting a person of honourable position.
2. Hwúi.

hausted my powers, there seems to be something standing straight up in front of me, and though I have the mind to make towards it I make no advance at all."

11. Once when the Master was seriously ill, Tsz-lu induced the other disciples to feign they were high officials acting in his service.—During a respite from his malady the Master exclaimed, "Ah! how long has Tsz-lu's conduct been false? Whom should *I* delude, if I were to pretend to have officials under me, having none? Should I deceive Heaven? Besides, were I to die, I would rather die in the hands of yourselves, my disciples, than in the hands of officials. And though I should fail to have a grand funeral over me, I should hardly be left on my death on the public highway, should I?"

12. Tsz-kung once said to him, "Here is a fine gem. Would you guard it carefully in a casket and store it away, or seek a good price for it and sell it?"

"Sell it, indeed," said the Master,—"that would I; but I should wait for the bidder."[1]

13. The Master protested he would "go and live among the nine wild tribes. "[2]

"A rude life," said some one;—"how could you put up with it?"

"What rudeness would there be," he replied, "if a 'superior man' was living in their midst?"

14. Once he remarked, "After I came back from Wei to Lu the music was put right, and each of the Festal Odes and Hymns was given its appropriate place and use."[3]

1. By the "fine gem" is said to have been meant the Master's own high qualification for official employment, which he seemed to set too little store upon. He sees the point in the question, and answers, "I will wait till I am asked."
2. By way of expressing his regret that his influence was so little among civilized folk.
3. The Festal Odes and Hymns are the contents of the *Shi-King*, *minus* the Ballads, &c., of the first part.

15. "Ah! which one of these following," he asked on one occasion, "are to be found (exemplified) in me,[1]—(proper) service rendered to superiors when abroad; duty to father and elder brother when at home; duty that shrinks from no exertion when dear ones die; and keeping free from the confusing effects of wine?"

16. Standing once on the bank of a mountain-stream, he said (musingly), "Like this are those that pass away—no cessation, day or night!"[2]

Other sayings:—

17. "I have not yet met with the man who loves Virtue as he loves Beauty.

1. Chinese commentators think the question, as in 3. 2, too self-depreciatory and make it mean, "What is there in me *besides* these?"
2. I give the ordinary meaning of the words; some native commentators make them allude to changes in mundane matters, or things of time, or of the "times"; and others take them as a hint to the disciples about unremitting study.

18. "Take an illustration from the making of a hill. A simple basketful is wanting to complete it, and the work stops. So I stop short.

"Take an illustration from the *levelling* of the ground. Suppose again just one basketful (is left), when the work has so progressed. There *I* desist![1]

19. "Ah! it was Hwúi, was it not? who, when I had given him his lesson, was the unflagging one!

20. "Alas for Hwúi! I saw him (ever) making progress. I never saw him stopping short.

21. "Blade, but no bloom,—or else bloom, but no produce;—ay, that is the way with some!

22. "Reverent regard is due to youth.[2] How know

---

1. Admonition to his students to persevere with their learning to its completion.
2. Almost exactly the *maxima debetur puero reverentia* of Juvenal.

we what difference there may be in them in the future from what they are now? Yet when they have reached the age of forty or fifty, and are still unknown in the world, then indeed they are no more worthy of such regard.

23. "Can any do otherwise than assent to words said to them by way of correction? Only let them reform by such advice, and it will then be reckoned valuable. Can any be other than pleased with words of gentle suasion? Only let them comply with them fully, and such also will be accounted valuable. With those who are pleased without so complying, and those who assent but do not reform, I can do nothing at all.

24. (1) "Give prominent place to loyalty and sincerity.
   (2) "Have no associates (in study) who are not (advanced) somewhat like yourself.

(3) "When you have erred, be not afraid to correct yourself.

25. "It may be possible to seize and carry off the chief commander of a large army,[1] but not possible so to rob one poor fellow of his will.

26. "One who stands,—clad in hempen robe, the worse for wear,—among others clad in furs of fox and badger, and yet unabashed;—'tis Tsz-lu, that, is it not?"

Tsz-lu used always to be humming over the lines—

> "From envy and enmity free,
> What deed doth he other than good? "[2]

"How should such a rule of life," asked the Master, "be *sufficient* to make any one good?"

1. Lit. three forces—each of 12,500 men.
2. *Shi-King*, I. iii. 8.

27. "When the year grows chilly, we know the pine and cypress are the last to fade.[1]

28. "The wise escape doubt; the good-hearted, trouble; the bold, apprehension.

29. "Some may study side by side, and yet be asunder when they come to the logic of things. Some may go on together in this latter course, but be wide apart in the standards they reach in it. Some, again, may together reach the same standard, and yet be diverse in weight (of character)."

30. "The blossom is out on the cherry tree,
        With a flutter on every spray.

1. Good men are like the evergreens.

Dost think that my thoughts go not out to thee?
Ah, why art thou far away!"[1]

(Commenting on these lines) the Master said "There can hardly have been much 'thought going out.' What does distance signify?"

1. From a spring-song—one of the pieces expurgated by Confucius from the collection out of which he compiled the *Shi-King*. The point of his little comment is not very clear.

Six

Confucius in private and official life—
Description of his habits, dress, diet, and
general deportment in various
circumstances.

1. In his own village, Confucius presented a somewhat plain and simple appearance, and looked unlike a man who possessed ability of speech.

But in the ancestral temple, and at Court, he spoke with the fluency and accuracy of a debater, but ever guardedly.

2. At Court, conversing with the lower order of great officials, he spoke somewhat firmly and directly; with those of the higher order his tone was somewhat more affable.

When the prince was present he was constrainedly reverent in his movements, and showed a proper degree of grave dignity in demeanour.

3. Whenever the prince summoned him to act as usher to the Court, his look would change somewhat, and he would make as though he were turning round to do obeisance.

He would salute those among whom he took up his position,[1] using the right hand or the left, and holding the skirts of his robe in proper position before and behind.—He would make his approaches with quick step, and with elbows evenly bent outwards.

When the visitor withdrew, he would not fail to report the execution of his commands, with the words, "The visitor no longer looks back."

4. When he entered the palace gate, it was with the body somewhat bent forward, almost as though he could not be admitted.—When he stood still, this would never happen in the middle of the gateway; nor when moving about would he ever tread on the

1. At the reception of a prince from another State there were *many* officials acting on behalf of host and guest, through whom ceremonial questions and answers were passed. Confucius was evidently at times required to act as one of these.

threshold.[1]—When passing the throne, his look would change somewhat, he would turn aside and make a sort of obeisance, and the words he spoke seemed as though he were deficient in utterance.

On going up the steps to the audience chamber, he would gather up with both hands the ends of his robe, and walk with his body bent somewhat forward, holding back his breath like one in whom respiration has ceased.—On coming out, after descending one step his countenance would relax and assume an appearance of satisfaction. Arrived at the bottom, he would go forward with quick step, his elbows evenly bent outwards, back to his position, constrainedly reverent in every movement.

5. When holding the sceptre[2] in his hand, his body would be somewhat bent forward, as if he were

1. This, and the centre of the gateway, were positions to be occupied only by the prince.
2. Here, the sceptre of the feudal prince. Confucius, when in

not equal to carrying it; wielding it now higher, as in a salutation,[1] now lower, as in the presentation of a gift; his look would also be changed and appear awestruck; and his gait would seem retarded, as if he were obeying some (restraining hand behind).

When he presented the gifts of ceremony,[2] he would assume a placid expression of countenance.

At the private interview he would be cordial and affable.

6. The good man would use no purple or violet colours for the facings of his dress.[3]

office, would carry it with him on occasion of embassages to neighbouring princes.

1. A Chinaman saluting clasps his *own* hands, holding them forward. In presenting a gift the hands are lower.
2. At the neighbouring prince's Court.
3. Because, it is said, such colours were adopted in fasting and mourning.

Nor would he have red or orange colour for his undress.[1]

For the hot season he wore a singlet, of either coarse or fine texture, but would also feel bound to have an outer garment covering it.

For his black robe he had lamb's wool; for his white one, fawn's fur; and for his yellow one, fox fur.[2]

His furred undress robe was longer, but the right sleeve was shortened.

He would needs have his sleeping-dress one and a half times his own length.

For ordinary home wear he used thick substantial fox or badger furs.

1. Because they did not belong to the five *correct* colours (viz. green, yellow, carnation, white and black), and were affected more by females.
2. The first was appropriate for wear at the Court of his own State; the second when at a neighbouring Court as envoy; the last in the ancestral temple.

When he left off mourning, he would wear all his girdle trinkets.

His kirtle in front, when it was not needed for full cover,[1] he must needs have cut down.

He would never wear his (black) lamb's-wool, or a dark-coloured cap, when he went on visits of condolence to mourners.[2]

On the first day of the new moon, he must have on his Court dress and to Court.

7. When observing his fasts, he made a point of having bright, shiny garments, made of linen.

He must also at such times vary his food, and move his seat to another part of his dwelling-room.

1. As at Court.
2. Since *white* was, as it is still, the mourning colour.

8. As to his food, he never tired of rice so long as it was clean and pure, nor of hashed meats when finely minced.

Rice spoiled by damp, and sour, he would not touch, nor tainted fish, nor bad meat, nor aught of a bad colour or smell, nor aught overdone in cooking, nor aught out of season.

Neither would he eat anything that was not properly cut, or that lacked its proper seasonings.

Although there might be an abundance of meat before him, he would not allow a preponderance of it to rob the rice of its beneficial effect in nutrition. Only in the matter of wine did he set himself no limit, yet he never drank so much as to confuse himself.

Tradesmen's wines, and dried meats from the market, he would not touch.

Ginger he would never have removed from the table during a meal.

He was not a great eater.

Meat from the sacrifices at the prince's temple he would never put aside till the following day. The meat of (his own) offerings he would never give out[1] after three days' keeping, for after that time none were to eat it.

At his meals he would not enter into discussions; and when reposing (afterwards) he would not utter a word.

Even should his meal consist only of coarse rice and vegetable broth or melons, he would make an offering,[2] and never fail to do so religiously.

9. He would never sit on a mat that was not straight.[3]

---

1. To kinsmen and friends.
2. The origin of meals being sacrificial, this the good man would do, somewhat as we say grace before meals.
3. Loving order in all things, his sense of order was disturbed in little matters as well as great.

10. After a feast among his villagers, he would wait before going away until the old[1] men had left.

When the village people were exorcising the pests,[2] he would put on his Court robes and stand on the steps of his hall (to receive them).

11. When he was sending a message of inquiry to a person in another State, he would bow twice[3] on seeing the messenger off.

Ki K'ang once sent him a present of some medicine. He bowed, and received it; but remarked,

1. Lit. those who carried a staff. Sexagenarians only were then, as in China now, supposed to use walking-sticks.
2. A new-year ceremony of expelling evil spirits and pestilential influences, consisting of a house to house visitation. Though silly and a little rowdy, the Sage would not disturb an old custom, but would seem to have encouraged it. During the recent plague in Hong Kong the Chinese requested permission for a special performance of this kind. It now consists mainly in processions, firing off crackers, &c.
3. The bowings being really intended for the person to whom the message was sent.

"Until I am quite sure of its properties I must not venture to taste it."

12. Once when the stabling was destroyed by fire, he withdrew from the Court, and asked, "Is any person injured?"—without inquiring as to the horses.

13. Whenever the prince sent him a present of food, he was particular to set his mat in proper order, and would be the first one to taste it. If the prince's present was one of raw meat, he must needs have it cooked, and make an oblation of it. If the gift were a live animal, he would be sure to keep it and care for it.

When he was in waiting, and at a meal with the prince, the prince would make the offering,[1] and he (the Master) was the pregustator.

When unwell, and the prince came to see him, he would arrange his position so that his head in-

1. The act of "grace," before eating.

clined towards the east, would put over him his Court robes, and draw his girdle across them.

When summoned by order of the prince, he would start off without waiting for his horses to be put to.

14. On his entry into the Grand Temple, he inquired about everything connected with its usages.

15. If a friend died, and there were no near relatives to take him to, he would say, "Let him be buried from my house."

For a friend's gift—unless it consisted of meat that had been offered in sacrifice—he would not bow, even if it were a carriage and horses.

16. In repose he did not lie like one dead. In his home life he was not formal in his manner.

Whenever he met with a person in mourning, even though it were a familiar acquaintance, he would be certain to change (his manner); and when he met with any one in full-dress cap, or with any blind person, he would also unfailingly put on a different look, even though he were himself in undress at the time.

In saluting any person wearing mourning he would bow forwards towards the front bar of his carriage; in the same manner he would also salute the bearer of a census-register.

When a sumptuous banquet was spread before him, a different expression would be sure to appear in his features, and he would rise up from his seat.[1]

At a sudden thunder-clap, or when the wind grew furious, his look would also invariably be changed.

17. On getting into his car, he would never fail (first) to stand up erect, holding on by the strap. When in the car, he would never look about, nor speak hastily, nor bring one hand to the other.

1. In acknowledgement of the generous hospitality.

18. "Let one but make a movement in his face,
And (the bird) will rise and seek (some safer) place."

Apropos of this, he said, "Here is a hen-pheasant from Shan Liang—and in season! and in season!" After Tsz-lu had got it prepared, he smelt it thrice, and then rose up from his seat.[1]

1. This whole paragraph is obscure, and the Chinese commentators differ in their explanations of it. I take the opening sentences as a quotation from some poem, in which evidently facial expression (which plays so large a part in the preceding paragraphs) is dwelt upon. "Shan Liang" is literally a mountain-bridge; but may it not be the name of some district or place? The Master's rising up from his seat must be taken, again, as expressive of his pleasure at having met with a luxury.

Seven

Comparative worth of certain disciples—
Death of the favourite one—Four of them
tell their wishes.

1. "The first to make progress in The Proprieties and in Music," said the Master, "are plain countrymen; after them, the men of higher standing.[1] If I had to employ any of them, I should stand by the former."

2. "Of those," said he, "who were about me when I was in the Ch'in and Ts'ai States, not one now is left to approach my door."

[2]*Note.*—The men of virtuous life were Yen Yuen (Hwúi), Min Tsz-k'ien, Yen Pih-niu, and Chung-kung (Yen Yung); the speakers and debaters were Tsai Wo and Tsz-kung; the (capable) government servants were Yen Yu and Tsz-lu; the literary students, Tsz-yu and Tsz-hiá.

1. Quite a different meaning is brought out by the native commentators, the chief of whom are followed by Prof. Legge; but I think they do violence to the plain text. They represent the whole paragraph as a quotation of a common saying about the men of former and later times.
2. Said to be an addition by the compilers.

3. "As for Hwúi," said the Master, "he is not one to help me on: there is nothing I say but he is not well satisfied with."[1]

4. "What a dutiful son was Min Tsz-k'ien!" he exclaimed. "No one finds occasion to differ from what his parents and brothers have said of him."

5. Nan Yung used to repeat three times over (the lines in the *Odes* about) the white sceptre.[2] Confucius caused his own elder brother's daughter to be given in marriage to him.

6. When Ki K'ang inquired which of the disciples were fond of learning, Confucius answered him,

1. He did not raise questions, see II. 9; and in *that* way did not lead him on into deeper discussions.
2. *Shi-King*, III. iii. 2—
"Flaws may be in thy white sceptre,
Yet they may be ground away;
Flaws in things that thou hast uttered—
All intangible are they!"

"There was one Yen Hwúi who was fond of it; but unfortunately his allotted time was short, and he died; and now his like is not to be found."

7. When Yen Yuen died, (his father) Yen Lu begged for the Master's carriage in order to get a shell for his coffin. "Ability or no ability," said the Master, "every father still speaks of 'my son.' When (my own son) Li died, and the coffin for him had no shell to it, (I know) I did not go on foot to get him one; but that was because I was (though retired) in the wake[1] of the ministers, and could not therefore well do so."

8. On the death of Yen Yuen the Master exclaimed, "Ah me! Heaven is ruining me, Heaven is ruining me!"

1. He was still about the Court when required for consultation; and was obliged to act as a high officer should. Yen Lu was not in such a position.

9. On the same occasion, his wailing for that disciple becoming excessive, those who were about him said, "Sir, this is too much!"—"Too much?" said he; "if I am not to do so for *him*, then—for whom else?"

10. The disciples then wished for the deceased a grand funeral. The Master could not on his part consent to this.[1] They nevertheless gave him one.— Upon this he remarked, "He used to look upon me as if I were his father. I could never, however, look on him as a son. 'Twas not my mistake, but yours, my children."

11. Tsz-lu propounded a question about ministering to the spirits (of the departed). The Master replied, "Where there is scarcely the ability to minis-

1. Because the family was very poor, and the grand funeral would involve them in expense.

ter to (living) men, how shall there be ability to minister to the spirits?"—On his venturing to put a question concerning death, he answered, "Where there is scarcely any knowledge about life, how shall there be any about death?"[1]

12. The disciple Min was by his side, looking affable and bland; Tsz-lu also, looking careless and intrepid; and Yen Yu and Tsz-kung, firm and precise. The Master was cheery.—"One like Tsz-lu there," (said he), "does not come to a natural end."[2]

13. Some persons in Lu were taking measures in regard to the Long Treasury House.—Min Tsz-k'ien observed, "How if it were (repaired) on the old lines?"—The Master upon this remarked, "This fellow is not a talker, but when he does speak he is bound to hit the mark!"

1. The answers *may* only have reference to the questioner.
2. Nor did he. He was killed during a rising in Wei.

14. "There is Yu's[1] harpsichord," exclaimed the Master—"what is it doing at my door?" On seeing, however, some disrespect shown to him by the other disciples, he added, "Yu has got as far as the top of the hall; only he has not yet entered the house."

15. Tsz-kung asked whether was the worthier of the two—Tsz-chang or Tsz-hiá. "The former," answered the Master, "goes beyond the mark; the latter falls short of it."

"So then Tsz-chang is the better of the two, is he?" said he.

"To go too far," he replied, "is about the same as to fall short."

16. The Chief of the Ki family was a wealthier man than the duke of Chow[2] had been, and yet Yen

1. Tsz-lu. A rebuke of his *style* of music seems to be intended. Yet the Master shows that he has made some progress, and will not have him contemned.
2. The example and "dream" of Confucius.

Yu gathered and hoarded for him, increasing his wealth more and more.

"He is no follower of mine," said the Master. "It would serve him right, my children, to sound the drum,[1] and set upon him."

17. [Characteristics of four disciples]:—
Tsz-káu was simple-minded; Tsang-sin, a dullard; Tsz-chang, full of airs; Tsz-lu, rough.

18. "As to Hwúi," said the Master, "he comes near to (perfection), while frequently in great want.— Tsz-kung does not submit to the appointments (of Heaven); and yet his goods are increased;—he is often successful in his calculations."

19. Tsz-chang wanted to know some marks of the (naturally) Good Man.[2]

1. Drums were sounded in the market-place to collect the people to witness the punishment of criminals.
2. This term was a technical one in the vocabulary of the Sage

"He does not walk in others' footprints," said the Master; "yet he does not get (beyond the hall) into the house."[1]

20. Once the Master said, "Because we allow that a man's words have something genuine in them, are they (necessarily) those of a superior man? or words carrying (only) an outward semblance and show of gravity?"

21. Tsz-lu put a question about the practice of precepts one has heard. The Master's reply was, "In a case where there is a father or elder brother still left with you, how should you practice all you hear?"

and his disciples, meaning, as the commentators say, a man constitutionally good, or having genius, without having studied.

1. I.e. He is not a copyist, and yet he never gets far forward. See, as to "the house," parag. 14.

"When, however, the same question was put to him by Yen Yu, his reply was, "Yes; do so."

Kung-si Hwa animadverted upon this to the Master. "Tsz-lu asked you, sir," said he, "about the practice of what one has learnt, and you said, 'There may be a father or elder brother still alive'; but when Yen Yu asked the same question, you answered, 'Yes, do so.' I am at a loss to understand you, and venture to ask what you meant."

The Master replied, "Yen Yu backs out of his duties; therefore I push him on. Tsz-lu has forwardness enough for them both; therefore I hold him back."

22. On the occasion of that time of fear in K'wang,[1] Yen Yuen having fallen behind, the Master said to him (afterwards), "I took it for granted you were a dead man." "How should I dare to die," said he, "while you, sir, still lived?"

1. See 5. 5.

23. On Ki Tsz-jen[1] putting to him a question anent Tsz-lu and Yen Yu, as to whether they might be called "great ministers," the Master answered, "I had expected your question, sir, to be about something extraordinary, and lo! it is only about these two.— Those whom we call 'great ministers' are such as serve their prince conscientiously, and who, when they cannot do so, retire. At present, as regards the two you ask about, they may be called '*qualified ministers*.'"

"Well, are they then," he asked, "such as will follow their leader?"

"They would not follow him who should slay his father and his prince!" was the reply.

24. Through the intervention of Tsz-lu, Tsz-káu was being appointed governor of Pi.[2]

1. Younger brother of the Chief of the Ki family. He had employed these two disciples in his service, hoping ultimately to get possession of the dukedom.
2. See on 2 7. Tsz-káu was only half-educated, simpleminded

104

"You are spoiling a (good) man's son," said the Master.

Tsz-lu rejoined, "But he will have the people and their superiors (to gain experience from), and there will be the altars;[1] what need to read books? He can become a student afterwards."[2]

"Here is the reason for my hatred of glib-tongued people," said the Master.

(see parag. 17), and quite unfit for such an office.

1. The Earth altar and Grain-god altar. He would have opportunities of worship.

2. A good story is given by Dr. Legge in a chapter on the disciples, corroborating what is here said about Tsz-lu. "At their first interview, the Master asked him what he was fond of, and he replied, 'My long sword.' Confucius said, 'If to your present ability there were added the results of learning, you would be a very superior man.' 'Of what advantage would learning be to me?' asked Tsz-lu. 'There is a bamboo ... which is straight itself without being bent. If you cut it down and use it, you can send it through a rhinoceros' hide;—what is the use of learning?' 'Yes,' said the Master, 'but if you feather it and point it with steel, will it not penetrate more deeply?' Tsz-lu bowed twice, and said, 'I will reverently receive your instructions.' "

25. On one occasion Tsz-lu, Tsăng Sih, Yen Yu, and Kung-si Hwa were sitting near him.

He said to them, "Though I may be a day older than you, do not (for the moment) regard me as such. While you are living this unoccupied life you are saying, 'We do not become known.' Now suppose some one got to know you, what then?"

Tsz-lu—first to speak—at once answered, "Give me a State of large size and armament,[1] hemmed in and hampered by other larger States, the population augmented by armies and regiments, causing a dearth in it of food of all kinds; give me charge of that State, and in three years' time I should make a brave country of it, and let it know its place."

The Master smiled at him.—"Yen," said he, "how would it be with you?"

"Give me," said Yen, "a territory of sixty or seventy *li*[2] square, or of fifty or sixty square; put me in

1. Lit. a State with 1000 war-chariots.
2. A *li* is about one-third of a mile. Either would be a small State.

106

charge of that, and in three years I should make the people sufficiently prosperous. As regards their knowledge of ceremonial or music, I should wait for superior men (to teach them that)."

"And with you, Kung-si, how would it be?"

This disciple's reply was, "I have nothing to say about my capabilities for such matters; my wish is to learn. I should like to be a junior assistant, in dark robe and cap, at the services of the ancestral temple, and at the Grand Receptions of the Princes by the Sovereign."

"And with you, Tsăng Sih?"

This disciple was strumming on his harpsichord, but now the twanging ceased, he turned from the instrument, rose to his feet, and answered thus: "Something different from the choice of these three." "What harm?" said the Master; "I want *each one* of you to tell me what his heart is set upon." "Well, then," said he, "give me—in the latter part of spring—dressed in full spring-tide attire—in company with five or six young fellows of twenty,[1] or six or seven lads under that age, to do the ablutions in the *I* stream, enjoy a breeze in the raindance,[2] and finish up with songs on the road home."

The Master drew in his breath, sighed, and exclaimed, "Ah, I take with you!"

The three other disciples having gone out, leaving Tsăng Sih behind, the latter said, "What think you of the answers of those three?"—"Well, each told me what was uppermost in his mind," said the Master;—"simply that."

"Why did you smile at Tsz-lu, sir?"

"I smiled at him because to have the charge of a State requires due regard to the Rules of Propriety, and his words betrayed a lack of modesty."

"But Yen, then—*he* had a State in view, had he not?"

1. Lit. capped ones. At twenty they underwent the ceremony of capping, and were considered *men*.
2. I. e. before the altars, where offerings were placed with prayer for rain. A religious dance.

"I should like to be shown a territory such as he described which does not amount to a State."

"But had not Kung-si also a State in view?"

"What are ancestral temples and Grand Receptions, but for the feudal lords (to take part in)?[1] If Kung-si were to become an unimportant assistant at these functions, who could become an important one?"

1. The princes were themselves the attendants of the sovereign in the ancestral temple. See the *Shi-King*, IV. i. 1 and 4; IV. ii. 7 and 8.

Eight

The Master's answers when consulted
about fellow-feeling, the superior man,
enlightenment, government, litigations—
Virtue, vice, and illusions—
Philanthropy—Friendships.

1. Yen Yuen was asking about man's proper regard for his fellow-man. The Master said to him, "Self-control, and a habit of falling back upon propriety, (virtually) effect it. Let these conditions be fulfilled for one day, and every one round[1] will betake himself to the duty. Is it to begin in oneself, or think you, indeed! it is to begin in others?"

"I wanted you to be good enough," said Yen Yuen, "to give me a brief synopsis of it."

Then said the Master, "Without propriety use not your eyes; without it use not your ears, nor your tongue, nor a limb of your body."

"I may be lacking in diligence," said Yen Yuen, "but with your favour I will endeavour to carry out this advice."

2. Chung-kung asked about man's proper regard for his fellows.

1. 天下, the empire, the world, here *tout le monde.*

To him the Master replied thus:—"When you go forth from your door, be as if you were meeting some guest of importance. When you are making use of the common people (for State purposes), be as if you were taking part in a great religious function. Do not set before others what you do not desire yourself. Let there be no resentful feelings against you when you are away in the country, and none when at home."

"I may lack diligence," said Chung-kung, "but with your favour I will endeavour to carry out this advice."

3. Sz-ma Niu[1] asked the like question. The answer he received was this:—"The words of the man who has a proper regard for his fellows are uttered with difficulty."

1. Another disciple. Each seems to have been answered according to his ability or character.

" 'His words—uttered with difficulty?' " he echoed (in surprise). "Is that what is meant by proper regard for one's fellow-creatures?"

"Where there is difficulty in *doing*," the Master replied, "will there not be some difficulty in *utterance*?"

4. The same disciple put a question about the "superior man."—"Superior men," he replied, "are free from trouble and apprehension."

" 'Free from trouble and apprehension!' " said he. "Does *that* make them 'superior men'?"

The Master added, "Where there is found, upon introspection, to be no chronic disease, how shall there be any trouble? how shall there be any apprehension?"

5. The same disciple, being in trouble, remarked, "I am alone in having no brother, while all else have theirs—younger or elder."

Tsz-hiá said to him, "I have heard this:[1] 'Death and life have destined times; wealth and honours rest with Heaven. Let the superior man keep watch over himself without ceasing, showing deference to others, with propriety of manners,—and all within the four seas[2] will be his brethren. How should he be distressed for lack of brothers!' "

6. Tsz-chang asked what (sort of man) might be termed "enlightened."

The Master replied, "That man, with whom drenching slander and cutting calumny gain no currency, may well be called enlightened. Ay, he with whom such things make no way may well be called enlightened in the extreme."[3]

1. From Confucius, it is generally thought.
2. The supposed boundaries of the earth; but evidently, as in the *Shi-King*, IV. v. 3, a *meiosis* for the empire.
3. This is no proper answer, but it had doubtless reference to some circumstances unmentioned.

7. Tsz-kung put a question relative to govern-ment.—In reply the Master mentioned (three essen-tials):—sufficient food, sufficient armament, and the people's confidence.

"But," said the disciple, "if you cannot really have all three, and one has to be given up, which would you give up first?"

"The armament," he replied.

"And if you are obliged to give up one of the re-maining two, which would it be?"

"The food," said he. "Death has been the portion of all men from of old. Without the people's trust nothing can stand."

8. Kih Tsz-shing[1] once said, "Give me the inborn qualities of a gentleman, and I want no more. How are such to come from book-learning?"

Tsz-kung exclaimed, "Ah! sir, I regret to hear such words from you. A gentleman!—But 'a team

1. A great officer of the State of Wei.

117

of four can ne'er o'ertake the tongue!' Literary accomplishments are much the same as inborn qualities, and inborn qualities as literary accomplishments. A tiger's or leopard's skin without the hair might be a dog's or sheep's when so made bare."

9. Duke Ngai was consulting Yu Joh.[1] Said he, "It is a year of dearth, and there is an insufficiency for Ways and Means,—what am I to do?"

"Why not apply the Tithing Statute?"[2] said the minister.

"But two tithings would not be enough for my purposes," said the duke; "what would be the good of applying the Statute?"

The minister replied, "So long as the people have enough (left for themselves), who of them will allow their prince to be without enough? But—

1. A former disciple of Confucius now a minister of Lu.
2. On the Royal Tenths, see *Shi-King*, II. vi. 7.

when the people have not enough, who will allow their *prince* all that he wants?"

10. Tsz-chang was asking how the standard of virtue was to be raised, and how to discern what was illusory or misleading. The Master's answer was, "Give a foremost place to honesty and faithfulness, and tread the path of righteousness, and you will raise the standard of virtue. As to discerning what is illusory, here is an example of an illusion:—Whom you love you wish to live; whom you hate you wish to die. To have wished the same person to live and also to be dead,—there is an illusion for you."

11. Duke King of Ts'i consulted Confucius about government.—His answer was, "Let a prince be a prince, and ministers be ministers; let fathers be fathers, and sons be sons."

"Good!" exclaimed the duke; "truly if a prince fail to be a prince, and ministers to be ministers, and if fathers be not fathers, and sons not sons, then, even though I may have my allowance of grain,[1] should I ever be able to relish it?"

12. "The man to decide a cause[2] with half a word," exclaimed the Master, "is Tsz-lu!"

Tsz-lu never let a night pass between promise and performance.[3]

13. "In *hearing* causes, I am like other men," said the Master. "The great point is—to *prevent* litigation."

14. Tsz-chang having raised some question about government, the Master said to him, "In the settlement of its (principles) be unwearied; in its administration—see to that loyally."

1. I.e. revenue, or personal allowance from the State.
2. Tsz-lu was now a magistrate.
3. Dr. Legge's rendering of 無宿諾 is perhaps happier: "Never slept over a promise."

15. "The man of wide research," said he, "who also restrains himself by the Rules of Propriety, is not likely to transgress."

16. Again, "The noble-minded man makes the most of others' good qualities, not the worst of their bad ones. Men of small mind do the reverse of this."

17. Ki K'ang was consulting him about the direction of public affairs. Confucius answered him, "A director should be (himself) correct.[1] If you, sir, as a *leader* show correctness, who will dare not to be correct?"

18. Ki K'ang, being much troubled on account of robbers abroad, consulted Confucius on the matter. He received this reply: "If you, sir, were not covetous,

1. 政者正, *ching che ching.* There is evidently a play on the words. *Ching,* to direct or govern, is pronounced exactly like *ching,* correct.

neither would they steal, even were you to bribe them to do so."[1]

19. Ki K'ang, when consulting Confucius about the government, said, "Suppose I were to put to death the disorderly for the better encouragement of the orderly;—what say you to that?"

"Sir," replied Confucius, "in the administration of government why resort to capital punishment? Covet what is good, and the people will be good. The virtue of the noble-minded man is as the wind, and that of inferior men as grass; the grass must bend, when the wind blows upon it."

20. Tsz-chang asked how (otherwise) he would describe the learned official who might be termed influential.

---

1. This man had usurped the headship of the Ki family, and had carried off the child who was the rightful heir.

"What, I wonder, do you mean by one who is influential?" said the Master.

"I mean," replied the disciple, "one who is sure to have a reputation throughout the country, as well as at home."

"That," said the Master, "is reputation, not influence. The influential man, then, if he be one who is genuinely straightforward and loves what is just and right, a discriminator of men's words, and an observer of their looks, and in honour careful to prefer others to himself,—will certainly have influence, both throughout the country and at home.— The man of (mere) reputation, on the other hand, who speciously affects philanthropy, though in his way of procedure he acts contrary to it, while yet quite evidently engrossed with that virtue,—will certainly have reputation, both in the country and at home."

21. Fan Ch'i, strolling with him over the ground below the place of the rain-dance, said to him, "I

venture to ask how to raise the standard of virtue, how to reform dissolute habits, and how to discern what is illusory?"

"Ah! a good question indeed!" he exclaimed. Well, is not putting duty first, and success second, a way of raising the standard of virtue? And is not attacking the evil in oneself, and not the evil which is in others, a way of reforming dissolute habits? And as to illusions, is not one morning's fit of anger, causing a man to forget himself, and even involving in the consequences those who are near and dear to him,—is not that an illusion?"

22. The same disciple asked him what was meant by "a right regard for one's fellow-creatures."[1] He replied, "It is love to man."

Asked by him again what was meant by wisdom, he replied, "It is knowledge of man."

Fan Ch'i did not quite grasp his meaning.

1. 仁. Here the Master is quite explicit in his reply.

The Master went on to say, "Lift up the straight, set aside the crooked, so can you make the crooked straight."

Fan Ch'i left him, and meeting with Tsz-hiá he said, "I had an interview just now with the Master, and I asked him what wisdom was. In his answer he said, 'Lift up the straight, set aside the crooked, and so can you make the crooked straight.' What was his meaning?"

"Ah! words rich in meaning, those," said the other. "When Shun was emperor, and was selecting his men from among the multitude, he 'lifted up' Káu-yáu; and men devoid of right feelings towards their kind went far away. And when T'ang was emperor, and chose out his men from the crowd, he 'lifted up' I-yin,—with the same result."[1]

1. The former was made Minister of Crime and Controller of the frontier tribes, and it is chiefly to him that the glories of Shun's reign are attributed. The latter was T'ang's prime minister, and he is spoken of as the destroyer of the Hiá dynasty and founder of the Shang (or Yin).

23. Tsz-kung was consulting him about a friend. "Speak to him frankly, and respectfully," said the Master, "and gently lead him on. If you do not succeed, then stop; do not submit yourself to indignity."

24. The learned Tsăng observed, "In the society of books the 'superior man' collects his friends; in the society of his friends he is furthering goodwill among men."

Nine

More answers on the art of governing—
How to deal with dense populations—
Different estimates of
"straightforwardness"—The social virtue
again—Qualifications for office—
Consistency—The superior man—
How to prepare the people
to defend their country.

1. Tsz-lu was asking about government. "Lead the way in it," said the Master, "and work hard at it."

Requested to say more, he added, "And do not tire of it."

2. Chung-kung, on being made first minister to the Chief of the Ki family, consulted the Master about government, and to him he said, "Let the heads of offices *be* heads. Excuse small faults. Promote men of sagacity and talent."

"But," he asked, "how am I to know the sagacious and talented, before promoting them?"

"Promote those whom you do know," said the Master. "As to those of whom you are uncertain, will *others* omit to notice them?"

3. Tsz-lu said to the Master, "As the prince of Wei, sir, has been waiting for you to act for him in his government, what is it your intention to take in hand first?"

"One thing of necessity," he answered,—"the rectification of terms."[1]

"That!" exclaimed Tsz-lu. "How far away you are, sir! Why such rectification?"

"What a rustic you are, Tsz-lu!" rejoined the Master. "A gentleman would be a little reserved and reticent in matters which he does not understand.—If terms be incorrect, language will be incongruous; and if language be incongruous, deeds will be imperfect.—So, again, when deeds are imperfect, propriety and harmony cannot prevail, and when this is the case laws relating to crime will fail in their aim; and if these last so fail, the people will not know where to set hand or foot.—Hence, a man of superior mind, certain first of his terms, is fitted to speak; and being certain of what he says can proceed upon it. In the language of such a per-

1. See 8 .11: "Let a prince be a prince," &c.

son there is nothing *heedlessly irregular*,—and that is the sum of the matter."

4. Fan Ch'i requested that he might learn something of husbandry. "(For *that*)" said the Master, "I am not equal to an old husbandman." Might he then learn something of gardening? he asked. "I am not equal to an old gardener,"[1] was the reply.

"A man of little mind, that!" said the Master, when Fan Ch'i had gone out. "Let a man who is set over the people love propriety, and they will not presume to be disrespectful. Let him be a lover of righteousness, and they will not presume to be aught but submissive. Let him love faithfulness and truth, and they will not presume not to lend him their hearty assistance. Ah, if all this only *were* so,

---

1. A commentator (Yen Ts'an) gives the proverb, "About ploughing ask the labourer, about weaving ask the maid."

the people from all sides would come to such a one, carrying their children on their backs. What need to turn his hand to husbandry?"

5. "Though a man," said he, "could hum through the *Odes*—the three hundred—yet should show himself unskilled when given some administrative work to do for his country; though he might know *much* (of that other lore), yet if, when sent on a mission to any quarter, he could answer no question personally and unaided, what after all is he good for?"

6. "Let (a leader)," said he, "show rectitude in his own personal character, and even without directions from him things will go well. If he be not personally upright, his directions will not be complied with."

7. Once he made the remark, "The governments of Lu and of Wei are in brotherhood."[1]

1. The States had been held at the beginning of the dynasty by

8. Of King, a son of the duke of Wei, he observed that "he managed his household matters well. On his coming into possession, he thought, 'What a strange conglomeration!'—Coming to possess a little more, it was, 'Strange, such a result!' And when he became wealthy, 'Strange, such elegance!' "[1]

9. The Master was on a journey to Wei, and Yen Yu was driving him.—"What multitudes of people!" he exclaimed. Yen Yu asked him, "Seeing they are so numerous, what more would you do for them?"

"Enrich them," replied the Master.[2]

two brothers, and they had now fared much in the same way for centuries.
1. His excellent management is to be seen in his gradual prosperity, but his indifference about wealth is noted at the various stages of it.
2. We find Mencius inculcating the same ideas. How true they are! The first thing is to raise the material welfare of a people; they will then, says Mencius, "have a fixed heart"; and it will be easier to raise their morals. "Wealth," says Mr. Danson (*Wealth of Households*, Clarendon Press), "is not virtue; but it tends to make virtue easy. . . . To use it well is to elevate in the

"And after enriching them, what more would you do for them?"

"Instruct them."

10. "Were any one (of our princes) to employ me," he said, "after a twelvemonth I might have made some tolerable progress; but give me three years, and my work should be done."

11. Again, "How true is that saying, 'Let good men have the management of a country for a century, and they would be adequate to cope with evil-doers, and thus do away with capital punishments.' "

12. Again, "Suppose (the ruler) to possess true kingly qualities, then surely after one generation[1] there would be good-will among men."

scale of being all over whom we have influence. . . . We must needs think of 'the Good Samaritan' as of one who had pence to spare."
1. The Chinese reckon a generation 世 at 30 years.

13. Again, "Let a ruler but see to his own rectitude, and what trouble will he then have in the work before him? If he be unable to rectify himself, how is he to rectify others?"

14. Once when Yen Yu was leaving the Court, the Master accosted him. "Why so late?" he asked. "Busy with legislation," Yen replied. "The details[1] of it," suggested the Master; "had it been legislation, I should have been there to hear it, even though I am not in office."

15. Duke Ting asked if there were one sentence which (if acted upon) might have the effect of making a country prosperous.

1. Yen Yu was in the service of the ambitious Chief of the Ki family, about whose usurpations of royal prerogatives see on Book III. 1, 2, 6. The Master thought that business there should be executive rather than legislative. The commentators, however, suppose he meant the family affairs.

Confucius answered, "A sentence could hardly be supposed to do so much as that. But there is a proverb people use which says, "To play the prince is hard, to play the minister not easy." Assuming that it is *understood* that "to play the prince is hard," would it not be *probable* that with that one sentence the country should be made to prosper?"

"Is there, then," he asked, "one sentence which (if acted upon) would have the effect of ruining a country?"

Confucius again replied, "A sentence could hardly be supposed to do so much as that. But there is a proverb men have which says, 'Not gladly would I play the prince, unless my words were ne'er withstood.' Assuming that the (words) were good, and that none withstood them, would not that also be good? But assuming that they were *not* good, and yet none withstood them, would it not be probable that with that one saying he would work his country's ruin?"

16. When the duke of Shĕh consulted him about government, he replied, "Where the *near* are gratified, the *far* will follow."

17. When Tsz-hiá became governor of Kü-fu, and consulted him about government, he answered, "Do not wish for speedy results. Do not look at trivial advantages. If you wish for speedy results, they will not be far-reaching; and if you regard trivial advantages you will not successfully deal with important affairs."

18. The duke of Shĕh in a conversation with Confucius said, "There are some straightforward persons in my neighbourhood. If a father have stolen a sheep, the son will give evidence against him."

"Straightforward people in my neighbourhood are different from those," said Confucius. "The father will hold a thing secret on his son's behalf, and the son does the same for his father. They are on their *way* to becoming straightforward."[1]

19. Fan Ch'i was asking him about duty to one's fellow-men. "Be courteous," he replied, "in your private sphere; be serious in any duty you take in hand to do; be leal-hearted in your intercourse with others. Even though you were to go amongst the wild tribes, it would not be right for you to neglect these duties."

20. In answer to Tsz-kung, who asked "how he would characterize one who could fitly be called 'learned official'? the Master said, "He may be so called who in his private life is affected with a sense of his own unworthiness, and who, when sent on a mission to any quarter of the empire, would not disgrace his prince's commands."

1. Or, Straightforwardness *lies in their way* 在其中.

"May I presume," said his questioner, "to ask what sort you would put next to such?"

"Him who is spoken of by his kinsmen as a dutiful son, and whom the folks of his neighbourhood call 'good brother.' "

"May I still venture to ask whom you would place next in order?"

"Such as are sure to be true to their word, and effective in their work—who are given to hammering, as it were, upon one note[1]—of inferior calibre indeed, but fit enough, I think, to be ranked next."

"How would you describe those who are at present in the government service?"

"Ugh! mere peck and panier[2] men! —not worth taking into the reckoning."

1. 硜硜然, *kang kang jen*, an expression borrowed from the monotonous beating of the musical stone.
2. The reference may be to their being mere measures of capacity. See on V. 3 and II. 2. Or, it may be, with more likelihood, mere food-getters; or, as Dr. Williams explains the phrase in his Dictionary, "rustics, who only know about eating."

21. Once he remarked, "If I cannot get *via media* men to impart (instruction) to, then I must of course take the impetuous and undisciplined![1] The impetuous ones will (at least) go forward and lay hold on things; and the undisciplined have (at least) something in them which needs to be brought out."[2]

22. "The Southerners," said he, "have the proverb, 'The man who sticks not to rule will never make a charm-worker or a medical man.'[3] Good!— 'Whoever is intermittent in his practice of virtue will live to be ashamed of it' "[4] "Without *prognostication*," he added, "that will indeed be so."

1. Or, the wild and the playful—in the first sense applied to dogs.
2. Lit. which they do not do.
3. There would be little difference between these professions then, and they are not much unlike now.
4. This sentence is from the *Book of Changes*—the 恆, *hang*, diagram.

23. "The nobler-minded man," he remarked, "will be agreeable even when he disagrees; the small-minded man will agree and be disagreeable."

24. Tsz-kung was consulting him, and asked, "What say you of a person who was liked by all in his village?"

"That will scarcely do," he answered.

"What, then, if they all *dis*liked him?"

"That, too," said he, "is scarcely enough. Better if he were liked by the *good* folk in the village, and disliked by the *bad*."

25. "The superior man," he once observed, "is easy to serve, but difficult to please. Try to please him by the adoption of wrong principles, and you will fail. Also, when such a one employs others, he uses them according to their capacity.—The inferior man is, on the other hand, difficult to serve, but easy to please. Try to please *him* by the adoption of

141

wrong principles, and you will succeed. And when *he* employs others he requires them to be fully prepared (for everything)."

26. Again, "The superior man can be high without being haughty. The inferior man can be haughty if not high."

27. "The firm, the unflinching, the plain and simple, the slow to speak," said he once, "are approximating towards their duty to their fellowmen."

28. Tsz-lu asked how he would characterize one who might fitly be called an educated gentleman. The Master replied, "He who can properly be so called will have in him a seriousness of purpose, a habit of controlling himself, and an agreeableness of manner: among his friends and associates the seri-

ousness and the self-control, and among his brethren the agreeableness of manner."[1]

29. "Let good and able men discipline[2] the people for seven years," said the Master, "and after that they may do to go to war."

30. But said he, "To lead an undisciplined[3] people to war—*that* I call throwing them away."

1. Poor Tsz-lu was wanting in all these qualifications, and the reply was, as usual, limited to what *he* had yet to learn.
2. In both cases more is meant than merely military instruction and discipline: it is general instruction. But how must the Chinese regard the sayings, after recent experience!
3. See note 2, p. 93.

Ten

Good and bad government—Superior
men and humaneness—Miscellaneous
sayings—Estimate of historical
characters—Murder of a duke—The
superior man—Returning good for evil—
Worthies retiring from the world—A
king's mourning—A renegade disciple—A
precocious youth.

145

1. Yuen Sz[1] asked what might (be considered to) bring shame on one.

"Pay," said the Master; "pay—(ever looking to that), whether the country be well or badly governed."

2. "When imperiousness, boastfulness, resentments, and covetousness cease to prevail (among the people), may it be considered that mutual good-will has been effected?"—To this question the Master replied, "A hard thing (overcome) it may be considered. But as to the mutual good-will—I cannot tell."

3. "Learned officials," said he, "who hanker after a home life, are not worthy of being esteemed as such."

1. A former disciple, now in office.

4. Again, "In a country under good government, speak boldly, act boldly. When the land is ill-governed, though you act boldly, let your words be moderate."

5. Again, "Men of virtue will needs be men of words [i. e. will speak out], but men of words are not necessarily men of virtue. They who care for their fellow-men will needs be bold, but the bold may not necessarily be such as care for their fellow-men."

6. Nan-kung Kwoh, who was consulting Confucius, observed respecting *I*, the skilful archer, and Ngau, who could propel a boat on dry land,[1] that neither of them died a natural death; while Yu and Tsih,[2] who with their own hands had laboured at husbandry, came to wield imperial sway.

1. Both belonged to the ancient legendary period.
2. On Yu, see 4 21. On Tsih, see *Shi-king*, III. ii. 1, for a full account.

The Master gave him no reply.[1] But when the speaker had gone out he exclaimed, "A superior man, that! A man who values virtue, that!"

7. "There have been noble-minded men," said he, "who yet were wanting in philanthropy; but never has there been a small-minded man who had philanthropy in him."

8. He asked, "Can any one refuse to toil for those he loves? Can any one to *exhort*, who is true-hearted?"

9. Speaking of the preparation of Government Notifications (in his day) he said, "P'i would draw

1. From modesty, it is thought, because the allusion to Yu and Tsih was taken as referring to Confucius himself, and the allusion to those who died violent deaths as referring to the men in power above him.

up a rough sketch of what was to be said; the Shi-shuh[1] then looked it carefully through and put it into proper shape; Tsz-yu next, who was master of the ceremonial of State intercourse, improved and adorned its phrases; and Tsz-ch'an of Tung-li added his scholarly embellishments thereto."

10. To some one who asked his opinion of the last-named,[2] he said, "He was a kind-hearted man."—Asked what he thought of Tsz-si,[3] he exclaimed, "Alas for him! alas for him!"—Asked again about Kwan Chung,[4] his answer was, "As to him, he

1. The third son and heir (?).
2. Prime minister of the State of Ch'ing. It is said that Confucius wept on hearing of his death. See more about his opinion of him, 1. 15.
3. Prime minister of the State of Tsu,—a double-minded man. He had used his influence against Confucius.
4. See on III. 22. His prince had allowed him to take the town as a reward for his services, and as a punishment to the other officer. Confucius sees more to commend in the sufferer.

once seized the town of P'in with its three hundred families from the Chief of the Pih clan, who, afterwards reduced to living upon coarse rice, with all his teeth gone, never uttered a word of complaint."

11. "It is no light thing," said he, "to endure poverty uncomplainingly; and no difficult thing to bear wealth without becoming arrogant."

12. Respecting Mang Kung-ch'oh,[1] he said that, while he was fitted for something better than the post of chief officer in the Chau or Wei families, he was not competent to act as minister in (small States like those of) T'ang or Sieh.

1. Chief of the Măng clan, a person for whom Confucius had a great regard; but he would not let that regard prevent him from estimating his abilities fairly. The Chau and Wei families, and one other, shared between them the government of the State of Tsin, so the work was slight.

13. Tsz-lu asked how he would describe a perfect man. He replied, "Let a man have the sagacity of Tsang Wu-chung,[1] the freedom from covetousness of Kung-ch'oh,[2] the boldness of Chwang[3] of Pĭn, and the attainments in polite arts of Yen Yu;[4] and gift him further with the graces taught by the *Books of Rites* and *Music*—then he may be considered a perfect man.—But," said he, "what need of such in *these* days? The man that may be regarded as perfect (now) is the one who, seeing some advantage to himself, is mindful of righteousness; who, seeing danger, risks his life; and who, if bound by some covenant of long standing, never forgets its conditions as life goes on."

1. An officer of Lu, not long dead, who had acquired the reputation of a sage.
2. The person named in full in last paragraph.
3. An official who seems to have been an intrepid tiger-hunter.
4. A disciple.

14. Respecting Kung-shuh Wăn,[1] the Master inquired of Kung-ming Kiá,[2] saying, "Is it true that your master never speaks, never laughs, never takes (aught from others)?"

"Those who told you that of him," said he, "have gone too far. My master speaks when there is occasion to do so, and men are not surfeited with his speaking. When there is occasion to be merry too, he will laugh, but men have never overmuch of his laughing. And whenever it is just and right to take (things from others), he will take them, but never so as to allow men to think him burdensome."

"Is that the case with him?" said the Master. "Can it be so?"

15. Respecting Tsang Wu-chung [see 13], the Master said, "When he sought from Lu the appoint-

---

1. A great statesman in Wei.
2. "A man of Wei" is all the commentaries say of him.

ment of a successor to him, and for this object held on to his possession of (the fortified city of) Fang—if you say he was not then using constraint towards his prince, I must refuse to believe it."

16. Duke Wăn of Tsin he characterized as "artful but not upright"; and duke Hwan of Ts'i as "upright but not artful."[1]

17. Tsz-lu remarked, "When duke Hwan caused his brother Kiu to be put to death, Sháu Hwuh committed suicide, but Kwan Chung did not.[2] I should say he was not a man who had much good-will in him—eh?"

1. Both lived in the seventh century B. C.
2. Hereby hangs a tale. The two brothers were refugees during a time of disturbance in their own State, and Kiu, the younger, was in Lu, accompanied by the two ministers Sháu Hwuh and Kwan Chung. On the death of their father, Hwan returned first to his home, took possession, and caused his brother—still in Lu—to be put to death. One of his attendant ministers (Sháu) died with him

The Master replied, "When duke Hwan held a great gathering of the feudal lords, dispensing with military equipage, it was owing to Kwan Chung's energy that such an event was brought about. Match such good-will as that—match it if you can."

18. Tsz-kung then spoke up. "But *was* not Kwan Chung wanting in good-will? *He* could not give up his life when duke Hwan caused his brother to be put to death. Besides, he became the duke's counsellor."

"And in acting as his counsellor put him at the head of all the feudal lords," said the Master, "and unified and reformed the whole empire; and the people, even to this day, reap benefit from what he did. Had it not been for him we should have been going about with locks unkempt and buttoning our

by his own hand, and the other went back and served the surviving brother, in the end becoming very powerful in his influence over the whole empire. This was about B. C. 680.

jackets (like barbarians) on the left.—Would you suppose that he should show the same sort of attachment as exists between a poor yokel and his one wife—that he would asphyxiate himself in some sewer, leaving no one the wiser?"

19. Kung-shuh Wăn's[1] steward, (who became) the high officer Sien, went up accompanied by Wăn to the prince's hall of audience.[2]

When Confucius heard of this he remarked, "He may well be esteemed a 'Wăn.' "[3]

20. The Master having made some reference to the lawless ways of duke Ling of Wei, Ki K'ang said to him, "If he be like that, how is it he does not ruin his position?"

1. See on parag. 14.
2. I. e. his master recognizing his worth did not think it beneath his dignity to appear there in his company.
3. See on 1. 14 and 5. 5.

Confucius answered, "The Chung-shuh,[1] Yu, is charged with the entertainment of visitors and strangers; the priest T'o has charge of the ancestral temple; and Wang-sun Kiá has the control of the army and its divisions:—with men such as those, how should he come to ruin?"

21. He once remarked, "He who is unblushing in his words will with difficulty substantiate them."

22. Ch'in Shing had slain duke Kien.[2] (Hearing of this), Confucius, after performing his ablutions, went to Court and announced the news to duke Ngai, saying, "Ch'in Hăng[3] has slain his prince. May I request that you proceed against him?"

1. Some near relation of the duke. He was the same person as the Kung Wăn mentioned in 1. 14.
2. Prince of the State of Ts'i.
3. Another name for Ch'in Shing. He was one of duke Kien's own officers.

"Inform the Chiefs of the Three Families," said the duke.

(Soliloquizing upon this), Confucius said, "Since he uses me to back his ministers,[1] I did not dare not to announce the matter to him; and now he says, 'Inform the Three Chiefs.' "

He went to the Three Chiefs and informed them, but nothing could be done. (Whereupon again) he said, "Since he uses me to back his ministers, I did not dare not to announce the matter."

23. Tsz-lu was questioning him as to how he should serve his prince.—"Deceive him not, but reprove him," he answered.[2]

---

1. Confucius had now retired from office, and this incident occurred only two years before his death.
2. This evidently refers to some fatal measure devised by the prince, which Tsz-lu doubted whether he should openly combat, or secretly defeat.

24. "The minds of superior men," he observed, "trend upwards; those of inferior men trend downwards."

25. Again, "Students of old fixed their eyes upon themselves: *now* they learn with their eyes upon others."

26. Kü Pih-yuh[1] despatched a man with a message to Confucius. Confucius gave him a seat and among (other) inquiries he asked, "How is your master managing?" "My master," he replied, "has a great wish to be seldom at fault, and as yet he cannot manage it."

"What a messenger!" exclaimed he, (admiringly), when the man went out. "What a messenger!"

27. "When not occupying the office," was a remark of his, "devise not the policy."

1. A former disciple, now an officer in Wei.

28. The Learned Tsăng used to say, "The thoughts of the superior man do not wander from his own office."[1]

29. "Superior men," said the Master, "are modest in their words, profuse in their deeds."

30. Again, "There are three attainments of the superior man which are beyond me—the being sympathetic without anxiety, wise without scepticism, brave without fear."

"Sir," said Tsz-kung, "that is what *you* say of yourself."

31. Whenever Tsz-kung drew comparisons from others, the Master would say, "Ah, how wise and great you must have become! Now *I* have no time to do that."

1. This observation is plainly intended to illustrate the one next preceding. It is a quotation from the *Book of Changes*, LII. 3.

32. Again, "My great concern is, not that men do not know me, but that they *cannot*."[1]

33. Again, "If a man refrain from making preparations against his being imposed upon, and from counting upon others' want of good faith towards him, while he is foremost to perceive what is passing—surely that is a wise and good man."

34. Wi-shang Mau[2] accosted Confucius, saying, "K'iu, how comes it that you manage to go perching and roosting in this way? Is it not because you show yourself so smart a speaker, now?" "I should not dare do that," said Confucius. " 'Tis that I am sick of men's immoveableness and deafness to reason."

1. Or, it may be, "but that there is want of ability (in me to know them)." The phrase 患 其 不 能 is not quite clear.
2. A man of the town of Wu-Shing in Lu—evidently a person of importance and age. The "perching and roosting" refers to the Sage's visits to the different States.

35. "In a well-bred horse," said he, "what one admires is not its speed, but its good points."[1]

36. Some one asked, "What say you of (the remark), 'Requite enmity with kindness'?"[2]

"How then," he answered, "would you requite kindness?—Requite enmity with straightforwardness,[3] and kindness with kindness."

1. An illustration of what is most admirable in the "superior man."

2. Láu-tsz, the great philosopher and founder of a school of thought, contemporary with Confucius, had made this famous remark, 以 德 報 怨, see his *Táu Teh King*—translation by Dr. Chalmers (Trübner and Co.), p. 49.—I translate 怨 by "enmity," because that word and "resentment" and "murmuring" are the common meanings of the term throughout the book. Note that the same word occurs, translated "murmur," in the very next paragraph. 德, *teh*, the ordinary term for *virtue*, means any moral excellence or goodness, and here the Chinese commentators themselves explain it by benignity or kindness.

3. The word here is 直 = what is correct, straight, upright.

37. "Ah! no one knows me!" he once exclaimed.

"Sir," said Tsz-kung, "how comes it to pass that no one knows you?"

"While I murmur not against Heaven," continued the Master, "nor cavil at men; while I stoop to learn and aspire to penetrate into things that are high; yet 'tis Heaven alone knows what I am."

38. Liáu, a kinsman of the duke, having laid a complaint against Tsz lu before Ki K'ang, an officer[1] came (to Confucius) to inform him of the fact, and he added, "My lord is certainly having his mind poisoned by his kinsman Liáu, but through my influence perhaps we may yet manage to see him exposed[2] in the market-place or the Court."

"If right principles are to have their course, it is so destined," said the Master; "if they are *not* to have

1. I omit from the text his name, which was Tsz-fuh King-pih.
2. As a dead criminal!

their course, it is so destined. What can Liáu do against Destiny?"[1]

39. "There are worthy men," said the Master, "fleeing from the world; some from their district; some from the sight of men's looks; some from the language they hear."[2]

40. "The men who have risen (from their posts and withdrawn in this manner) are seven in number."

41. Tsz-lu, having lodged overnight in Shih-mun, was accosted by the gate-keeper in the morning. "Where from?" he asked. "From Confucius," Tsz-lu responded.—"That is the man," said he, "who knows things are not up to the mark, and is making some ado about them, is it not?"

1. "Destiny" here might be translated "Heaven's will," though the word is simply—"decree."
2. All directed against the misrule and manners of the times.

42. When the Master was in Wei, he was once pounding on the musical stone,[1] when a man[2] with a basket of straw crossed his threshold, and exclaimed, "Ah, there is a heart (that feels)! Ay, drub the stone!" After which he added, "How vulgar! how he hammers away on one note!—and no one knows him, and he gives up, and all is over!

'Be it deep, our skirts we'll raise to the waist,
—Or shallow, then up to the knee.' "[3]

"What determination!" said the Master. "Yet it was not hard to do."[4]

---

1. A suspended stone in shape like an inverted V.
2. Said in the commentaries to have been one of those worthies (parag. 39) who had fled from the world.
3. All these disjointed remarks would attract the attention of Confucius. Some were expressions of his own (XIII. 20; XIV. 37; V. 26; IX. 8), and the last two lines are from the *Shi-King*, I. iii. 9. The man had plainly once been a disciple.
4. Confucius now recognizes the man, and is surprised, and yet not much so, at what good men in such times would give up.

43. Tsz-chang once said to him, "In the *Book of the Annals* it is stated that while Káu-tsung[1] was in the Mourning Shed he spent the three years without speaking. What is meant by that?"

"Why must (you name) Káu-tsung?" said the Master. "It was so with all other ancient (sovereigns): when one of them died, the heads of every department agreed between themselves that they should give ear for three years to the Prime Minister."

44. "When their betters love the Rules, then the folk are easy tools," was a saying of the Master.[2]

45. Tsz-lu having asked what made a "superior man," he answered, "Self-culture, with a view to becoming seriously-minded."[3]

1. A king of the previous dynasty, known in the lists as Wu-ting. See *Shi-king*, IV. v. 3.
2. There are rhymes on the same words in the original, which look as if intentional.
3. The first reply is personal, as usual.

"Nothing more than that?" said he.

"Self-culture with a view to the greater satisfaction of others," added the Master.

"That, and yet no more?"

"Self-culture with a view to the greater satisfaction of all the clans and classes," he again added. "Self-culture for the sake of all—a result *that*, that would almost put Yáu and Shun[1] into the shade!"

46. To Yuen Jang,[2] who was sitting waiting for him in a squatting (disrespectful) posture, the Master delivered himself as follows:—"The man who in his youth could show no humility or subordination, who in his prime misses his opportunity, and who when old age comes upon him will not die—that man is a miscreant." And he tapped him on the shin with his staff.

1. Compare 2. 28.
2. A renegade, who had gone over to Láu-tsz's followers.

167

47. Some one asked about his attendant—a youth from the village of Kiueh—whether he was one who improved. He replied, "I note that he seats himself in the places (reserved for his betters), and that when he is walking he keeps abreast with his seniors.[1] He is not one of those who care for improvement: he wants to be a man all at once."

1. It is a habit with the Chinese, when a number are out walking together, for the eldest to go first,—the others tailing off according to their age. Many times I have seen this and wondered at it, and at the awkwardness in their conversation, till I knew the reason. It is a custom much older than the time of Confucius.

Eleven

Lessons of practical wisdom—The social
virtue again—Ancient precedents
for good government—Righteousness
an essential thing—The superior man—
Reciprocity the rule of life—Praise and
blame—Respect for what the majority
of the people like and dislike—Duty
and mercenary aims—Intellectual
attainments to be controlled
by "humanity"—Miscellaneous sayings—
Consideration for the blind.

1. Duke Ling of Wei was consulting Confucius about army arrangements. His answer was, "(Had you asked me about such things as) temple requisites,[1] I have learnt that business, but I have not yet studied military matters." And he followed up this reply by leaving on the following day.

(After this), during his residence in the State of Ch'in, his followers, owing to a stoppage of food-supply, became so weak and ill that not one of them could stand. Tsz-lu, with indignation pictured on his countenance, exclaimed, "And is a gentleman to suffer starvation?"

"A gentleman," replied the Master, "will endure it unmoved, but a common person breaks out into excesses under it."

1. Lit. vessels, on which the offerings were placed. He means that order, in more peaceful pursuits, was *his* object. The duke's favourite element was war.

2. Addressing Tsz-kung, the Master said, "You regard me as one who studies and stores up in his mind a multiplicity of things—do you not?"—"I do," he replied; "is it not so?"—"Not at all. I have *one* idea—one cord on which to string all."[1]

3. To Tsz-lu he remarked, "They who know Virtue are rare."

4. "(If you would know) one who without effort ruled well, was not Shun such a one? What did he indeed do? He bore himself with reverent dignity and undeviatingly 'faced the south,'[2] and that was all."

1. Man's heart is one thing, though its outgoings are many. The original is very terse 子 一 以 貫 之, and is, *verbatim*, "I unify by stringing them," the "stringing" process being borrowed from the stringing of copper cash, the coins of which are holed for the purpose.
2. The position of a sovereign.

5. Tsz-chang was consulting him about making way in life. He answered, "Be true and honest in all you say, and seriously earnest in all you do, and then, even if your country be one inhabited by barbarians, South or North, you will make your way. If you do not show yourself thus in word and deed how should you succeed, even in your own district or neighbourhood?—When you are afoot, let these two counsels be two companions preceding you, yourself viewing them from behind; when you drive, have them in view (as) on the yoke of your carriage. Then may you make your way."

Tsz-chang wrote them on the two ends of his cincture.

6. "Straight was the course of the Annalist Yu," said the Master—'ay, straight as an arrow flies; were the country well governed or ill governed, his was an arrow-like course.

"A man of masterly mind, (too), is Kü Pih-yuh! When the land is being rightly governed he will serve; when it is under bad government he is apt to recoil, and brood."[1]

7. "Not to speak to a man," said he, "to whom you ought to speak, is to lose your man; to speak to one to whom you ought not to speak is to lose your words. Those who are wise will not lose their man, nor yet their words."

8. Again, "The scholar whose heart is in his work, and who is philanthropic, seeks not to gain a livelihood by any means that will do harm to his philanthropy. There have been men who have destroyed their own lives in the endeavour to bring that virtue in them to perfection."

1. Both Yu and he were officials in Wei—the latter an old disciple.

9. Tsz-kung asked how to become philanthropic. The Master answered him thus: "A workman who wants to do his work well must first sharpen his tools.[1] In whatever land you live, serve under some wise and good man among those in high office, and make friends with the more humane of its men of education."

10. Yen Yuen consulted him on the management of a country. He answered:—

"Go by the Hiá Calendar.[2]

"Have the State carriages like those of the Yin[3] princes.

1. In view of what immediately follows, Dr. Legge aptly quotes a parallel from Prov. xxvii. 17: "Iron sharpeneth iron; so a man sharpeneth the countenance of his friend."
2. The year commenced in those old times in our February, at the earliest signs of Spring; but in Confucius' time it began two months earlier. This *dictum* of his caused a change in the next dynasty after the Chow, and is obeyed still.
3. The dynasty next before the Chow. The State carriages then were plain wooden ones; those of the Chow sovereigns were

"Wear the Chow cap.

"For your music let that of Shun be used for the posturers.

"Put away the songs of Ch'ing,[1] and remove far from you men of artful speech: the Ch'ing songs are immodest, and artful talkers are dangerous."

Other sayings of the Master:—

11. "They who care not for the morrow[2] will the sooner have their sorrow.

12. "Ah, 'tis hopeless! I have not yet met with the man who loves Virtue as he loves Beauty.

13. "Was not Tsang Wăn[3] like one who surreptitiously came by the post he held ? He knew the

gilded and decked out with gems.
1. *Shi-king*, I. vii. 2. Lit. distant.
3. See 1. 17

worth of Hwúi of Liu-hiá,[1] and could not stand in his presence.

14. "Be generous yourself, and exact little from others; then you banish complaints.

15. "With one who does not come to me inquiring 'What of this?' and 'What of that?' *I* never can ask 'What of this?' and give him up.

16. "If a number (of students) are all day together, and in their conversation never approach the subject of righteousness, but are fond merely of giving currency to smart little sayings, they are difficult indeed (to manage).

17. "When the 'superior man' regards righteousness as the thing material, gives operation to it according to the rules of propriety, lets it issue in

1. A high official in Lu about fifty years before Confucius.

humility, and become complete in sincerity,—there indeed is your superior man!

18. "The trouble of the superior man will be his own want of ability: it will be no trouble to him that others do not know him.

19. "Such a man thinks it hard to end his days and leave a name to be no longer named.

20. "The superior man is exacting of himself; the common man is exacting of others.

21. "A superior man has self-respect, and does not strive; is sociable, yet no party man.

22. "He does not promote a man because of his words, nor pass over the words because of the man."

23. Tsz-kung put to him the question, "Is there one word upon which the whole life may proceed?"

The Master replied, "Is not RECIPROCITY[1] such a word?—what you do not yourself desire, do not put before others."

24. "So far as I have to do with others, whom do I over-censure? whom do I over-praise? If there be something in them that looks very praiseworthy, that something I put to the test.—(I would have) the men of the present day to walk in the straight path whereby those of the Three Dynasties[2] have walked.

1. The word is 恕, *shu,* and this character is seen to be composed of 如 = *like,* and 心 = *heart;* whence one might expect *like-heartedness,* or *like-mindedness.* I render the word as Dr. Legge has done, but with a little hesitation. The dictionaries give the meaning as benevolence, forbearance, considerateness, sympathy, to excuse, to bear patiently, &c. The Chinese Imperial Dictionary gives it the verbal force of 仁.
2. The Hiá, Yin, and Chow; evidently the wise founders of these are meant.

25. "I have arrived as it were at the annalist's blank page.[1]—Once he who had a horse would lend it to another to mount; now, alas! it is not so.

26. "Artful speech is the confusion of Virtue. Impatience over little things introduces confusion into great schemes.

27. "What is disliked by the masses needs inquiring into; so also does that which they have a preference for.

28. "A man may give breadth to his principles: it is not principles (in themselves) that give breadth to the man.

29. "Not to retract after committing an error may itself be called error.

1. When the annalist was disgusted with current events, or in uncertainty about them, he would leave a blank to be filled up afterwards. So Confucius lamented the degeneracy of his times. The latter sentence in this paragraph is not quite clear.

30. "If I have passed the whole day without food and the whole night without sleep, occupied with my thoughts, it profits me nothing: I were better engaged in learning.

31. "The superior man deliberates upon how he may walk in truth, not upon what he may eat. The farmer may plough, and be on the way to want: the student learns, and is on his way to emolument. To live a right life is the concern of men of nobler minds: poverty gives them none.

32. "Whatsoever the intellect may attain to, unless the humanity[1] within is powerful enough to keep guard over it, is assuredly lost, even though it be gained.

"If there be intellectual attainments, and the humanity within *is* powerful enough to keep guard

1. The 仁. Intellectual attainments must be subservient to a right regard for others.

over them, yet, unless (in a ruler) there be dignity in his rule, the people will fail to show him respect.

"Again, given the intellectual attainments, and humanity sufficient to keep watch over them, and also dignity in ruling, yet if his movements be not in accordance with the Rules of Propriety, he is not yet fully qualified.

33. "The superior man may not be conversant with petty details, and yet may have important matters put into his hands. The inferior man may not be charged with important matters, yet may be conversant with the petty details.

34. "Good-fellowship is more to men than fire and water. I have seen men stepping into fire and into water, and meeting with death thereby; I have not yet seen a man die from planting his steps in the path of good-fellowship.

35. "Rely upon good-nature. 'Twill not allow precedence (even) to a teacher.

36. "The superior man is inflexibly upright, and takes not things upon trust.

37. "In serving your prince, make your service the serious concern, and let salary be a secondary matter.

38. "Where instruction is to be given, there must be no distinction of persons.[1]

39. "Where men's methods are not identical, there can be no planning by one on behalf of another.

40. "In speaking, perspicuity is all that is needed."

1. He made none in the case of his own son, and note thereon.

41. When the (blind)[1] music-master Mien paid him a visit, on his approaching the steps the Master called out "Steps," and on his coming to the mat[2] said "Mat." When all in the room were seated, the Master told him "So-and-so is here, so-and-so is here."

When the music-master had left, Tsz-chang said to him, "Is that the way to speak to the music-master?" "Well," he replied, "it is certainly the way to *assist* him."

1. The musicians at the Court were blind persons. See *Shi-king*, III. i. 8; IV. ii. 5. This incident is recorded immediately after the last paragraph, evidently not only to show the Sage's consideration for the blind, but to illustrate his sparing use of words.
2. For sitting upon,—as we should say "the chair."

Twelve

Against intestine strife—Supreme ruler
should never part with his authority—
Good and bad friendships—Errors to be
avoided by inferiors and superiors—
Classification of men as regards
knowledge—Nine things the superior
man should be mindful of—People's
opinion of wealth without virtue
and virtue without wealth—
Conversation between a disciple
and the son of Confucius.

1. The Chief of the Ki family was about to make an onslaught upon the Chuen-yu (domain).[1]

Yen Yu and Tsz-lu[2] in an interview with Confucius told him, "The Ki is about to have an affair with Chuen-yu."

"Yen," said Confucius, "does not the fault lie with you?—The Chief of Chuen-yu in times past was appointed lord of the East Mung (mountain);[3] besides, he dwells within the confines of (your own) State, and is an official of the State-worship;[4]—how can you think of making an onslaught upon him?"

"It is the wish of our Chief," said Yen Yu, "not the wish of either of us ministers."

1. A dependent territory in Lu. 2. Then in the Ki's service.
3. Presiding lord at its sacrifices, therefore a person of high authority and distinction. See a reference to this mountain in the *Shi-King*, IV. iv. 4.
4. A minister of the altars to Earth and the Grain-lord (Howtsih), and thus a minister of Lu.

187

Confucius said, "Yen, there is a sentence of Chau Jin[1] which runs thus: 'Having made manifest their powers and taken their place (in the official list), when they find themselves incompetent they resign; if they cannot be firm when danger threatens (the government), nor lend support when it is reeling, of what use then shall they be as Assistants?'—Besides, you are wrong in what you said. When a rhinoceros or tiger breaks out of its cage,—when a jewel or tortoise-(shell ornament) is damaged in its casket,—whose fault is it?"

"But," said Yen Yu, "so far as Chuen-yu is concerned, it is now fortified, and it is close to Pi; and if he does not now take it, in another generation it will certainly be a trouble to his descendants."

"Yen!" exclaimed Confucius, "it is a painful thing to a superior man to have to desist from saying, 'My wish is so-and-so,' and to be obliged to make

1. An ancient official annalist.

apologies. For my part, I have learnt this,—that rulers of States and heads of Houses are not greatly concerned about their small following, but about the want of equilibrium in it,—that they do not concern themselves about their becoming poor, but about the best means of living quietly and contentedly; for where equilibrium is preserved there will be no poverty, where there is harmony their following will not be small, and where there is quiet contentment there will be no decline nor fall.— Now if that be the case, it follows that if men in outlying districts are not submissive, then a reform in education and morals will bring them to; and when they have been so won, then will you render them quiet and contented.—At the present time you two are Assistants of your Chief; the people in the outlying districts are not submissive, and cannot be brought round. Your dominion is divided, prostrate, dispersed, cleft in pieces, and you as its guardians are powerless.—And plans are being

189

made for taking up arms against those who dwell within your own State. I am apprehensive that the sorrow of the Ki family is not to lie in Chuen-yu, but in those within their own screen."[1]

2. "When the empire is well ordered," said Confucius, "it is from the emperor[2] that edicts regarding ceremonial, music, and expeditions to quell (rebellion) go forth. When it is being ill governed, such edicts emanate from the feudal lords; and when the latter is the case, it will be strange if in ten generations there is not a collapse. If they emanate (merely) from the high officials, it will be strange if the collapse do not come in five generations. When the State-edicts are in the hands of the subsidiary ministers, it will be strange if in *three* generations there is no collapse.

1. I.e. in the consultations between the Chief and themselves.
2. Lit. the Son of Heaven.

"When the empire is well ordered, government is not (left) in the hands of high officials.

"When the empire is well ordered, the common people will cease to discuss (public matters)."

3. "For five generations," he said "the revenue has departed from the ducal household. Four generations ago the government fell into the hands of the high officials. Hence, alas! the straitened means of the descendants of the three Hwan (families)."[1]

4. "There are," said he, "three kinds of friendships which are profitable, and three which are detrimental. To make friends with the upright, with the trustworthy, with the experienced,[2] is to gain benefit; to make friends with the subtly perverse,

1. Three branches of the family of a former duke Hwan—of Lu.
2. Lit. those who have heard much, or learnt much.

with the artfully pliant, with the subtle in speech, is detrimental."

5. Again, "There are three kinds of pleasure which are profitable, and three which are detrimental. To take pleasure in going regularly through the various branches of Ceremonial and Music,[1] in speaking of others' goodness, in having many worthy wise friends, is profitable. To take pleasure in wild *bold* pleasures, in idling carelessly about, in the (too) jovial accompaniments of feasting, is detrimental."

6. Again, "Three errors there be, into which they who wait upon their superior may fall:—(1) to speak before the opportunity comes to them to speak, which I call heedless haste; (2) refraining from speaking when the opportunity has come,

1. The first as leading to propriety, the second as tending to general *bon accord*.

which I call concealment; and (3) speaking, regardless of the mood he is in,[1] which I call blindness."

7. Again, "Three things a superior should guard against:—(1) against the lusts of the flesh in his earlier years while the vital powers[2] are not fully developed and fixed, (2) against the spirit of combativeness when he has come to the age of robust manhood and when the vital powers are matured and strong, and (3) against ambitiousness when old age has come on and the vital powers have become weak and decayed."

8. "Three things also such a man greatly reveres:—(1) the ordinances of Heaven, (2) great men, (3) words of sages.—The inferior man knows not the ordinances of Heaven and therefore

1. Lit. without noticing the expression on his face.
2. Lit. blood and breath. This age is put down by one commentator as that below 29.

193

reveres them not, is unduly familiar in the presence of great men, and scoffs at the words of sages."

9. "They whose knowledge comes by birth are of all men the first (in understanding); they to whom it comes by study are next; men of poor intellectual capacity, who yet study, may be added as a yet inferior class; and lowest of all are they who are poor in intellect and never learn."

10. "Nine things there are of which the superior man should be mindful:—to be clear in vision, quick in hearing, genial in expression, respectful in demeanour, true in word, serious in duty, inquiring in doubt, firmly self-controlled in anger, just and fair when the way to success opens out before him."

11. "(Some have spoken of) 'looking upon goodness as upon something beyond their reach,' and of 'looking upon evil as like plunging one's hands into

scalding liquid';—I have seen the men, I have heard the sayings.

"(Some, again, have talked of) 'living in seclusion to work out their designs,' and of 'exercising themselves in righteous living in order to render their principles the more effective';—I have heard the sayings, I have not seen the men."

12. Duke King of Ts'i had his thousand teams of four, yet on the day of his death the people had nothing to say of his goodness. Pĕh-i and Shuh-ts'i[1] starved at the foot of Shau-yang, and the people make mention of them to this day.

> "E'en if not wealth thine object be,
> 'Tis all the same, thou'rt changed to me."[2]

"Is not this *à propos* in such cases?"

1. See on 1. 22.
2. *Shi-King*, II. iv. 4—concluding lines.

13. Tsz-k'in asked of Pih-yu,[1] "Have you heard anything else peculiar (from your father)?"

"Not yet," said he. "Once, though, he was standing alone when I was hurrying past him over the vestibule, and he said, 'Are you studying the *Odes*?' 'Not yet,' I replied. 'If you do not learn the *Odes*,' said he, 'you will not have the wherewithal for conversing.' I turned away and studied the *Odes*.—Another day, when he was again standing alone and I was hurrying past across the vestibule, he said to me, 'Are you learning the Rules of Propriety?' 'Not yet,' I replied. 'If you have not studied the Rules, you have nothing to stand upon,'[2] said he. I turned away and studied the Rules.—These two things I have heard from him."

---

1. The eldest son of Confucius, elsewhere (XI. 7) called Li. Li means a carp. Yu, in Pih-yu, also means a fish. The names were given him because at his birth the duke of Lu sent a present of a carp.
2. No stability: see VIII. 8.

Tsz-k'in turned away, and in great glee exclaimed, "I asked one thing, and have got three. I have learnt something, about the *Odes*, and about the Rules, and moreover I have learnt how the superior man will turn away[1] his own son."

14. The wife of the ruler of a State is called by her husband "(My) help-meet." She speaks of herself as "(Your) little handmaiden." The people of that State call her "The prince's help-meet," but addressing persons of another State they speak of her as "Our little princess."[2] When persons of another State name her they say also "(Your) prince's help-meet."

1. The commentator Yin says on this word 遠, "Confucius' instruction of his son was in no way different from his treatment of his disciples, hence this expression."

2. 寡 小 君, *K'wa siau Kiun;* the first character is almost untranslateable. It is used depreciatingly, and means *small,* almost like the next character, but is used by a sovereign in speaking of himself.

This paragraph may have been part of the Sage's instruction on the Proprieties, but there is nothing to show it.

Philosophy Books From Carol Publishing Group

The Age of Reason by Thomas Paine, paperback $8.95 (#50549)

Albert Einstein: Letters to Solovine, paperback $8.95 (#51422)

The Bertrand Russell Dictionary of Mind, Matter & Morals, paperback $9.95 (#51400)

The Book of Gandhi Wisdom, compiled by Trudy S. Settel, paperback $6.95 (#51622)

The Christ: A fundamental study of Christianity's early development by Charles Guignebert, paperback $9.95 (#51143)

The Creative Mind: An Introduction to Metaphysics by Henri Bergson, paperback $8.95 (#50421)

The Dark Side: Thoughts on the Futility of Life From Ancient Greeks to the Present by Alan R. Pratt, paperback $10.95 (#51481)

Deceptions and Myths of the Bible by Lloyd M. Graham, paperback $16.95 (#51124)

The Diary of Soren Kierkegaard, paperback $8.95 (#50251)

Einstein on Humanism, paperback $8.95 (#51436)

The Emotions: Outline of a Theory by Jean-Paul Sartre, paperback $5.95 (#50904)

Essays in Existentialism by Jean-Paul Sartre, paperback $12.95 (#50162)

The Ethics of Ambiguity by Simone de Beauvoir, paperback $9.95 (#50160)

The Ethics of Spinoza: The Road to Inner Freedom, by Baruch Spinoza, paperback $10.95 (#50536)

Existentialism and Human Emotions by Jean-Paul Sartre, paperback $7.95 (#50902)

The Great Secret: What is the meaning of life? by Maurice Maeterlinck, paperback $7.95 (#51155)

The Life and Major Writings of Thomas Paine, paperback $15.95 (#50414)

Literature & Existentialism by Jean-Paul Sartre, paperback $6.95 (#50105)

Martin Buber's Ten Rungs: Collected Hasidic Sayings, by Martin Buber, paperback $6.95 (#51593)

The Mystery-Religions and Christianity by Samuel Angus, paperback $9.95 (#51142)

Out of My Later Years by Albert Einstein, paperback $10.95 (#50357)

Philosophers of China: Classical and Contemporary by Clarence Burton Day, paperback $5.95 (#50622)

The Philosophy of Existentialism by Gabriel Marcel, paperback $8.95 (#50901)

The Psychology of Imagination by Jean-Paul Sartre, paperback $12.95 (#50305)

Rights of Man by Thomas Paine, paperback $9.95 (#50548)

The Sayings of Muhammad by Allama Sir-Abdullah Al-Mamum Al-Suhrawardy, paperback $7.95 (#51169)

The Theory of Relativity (and Other Essays) by Albert Einstein, paperback $8.95 (#51765)

The Way of Man: According to the Teaching of Hasidism, by Martin Buber, paperback $5.95 (#50024)

The World As I See It by Albert Einstein, paperback $7.95 (#50711)

Prices subject to change. Books subject to availability.